M000111497

the secrets to *Japanese* cooking

Use the Power of **Fermented Ingredients** to Create Authentic Flavors at Home

Shihoko Ura and Elizabeth McClelland
founders of Chopstick Chronicles

PAGE
PAGE STREET
PUBLISHING CO.

PAGE STREET
PUBLISHING CO.

Copyright © 2019 Shihoko Ura and Elizabeth McClelland

First published in 2019 by
Page Street Publishing Co.
27 Congress Street, Suite 105
Salem, MA 01970
www.pagestreetpublishing.com

All rights reserved. No part of this book may be reproduced or used, in any form or by any means, electronic or mechanical, without prior permission in writing from the publisher.

Distributed by Macmillan, sales in Canada by The Canadian Manda Group.

23 22 21 20 19   1 2 3 4 5

ISBN-13: 978-1-62414-783-8
ISBN-10: 1-62414-783-6

Library of Congress Control Number: 2018960859

Cover and book design by Ashley Tenn for Page Street Publishing Co.
Photography by Shihoko Ura
Cover image © Shihoko Ura

Printed and bound in China

Page Street Publishing protects our planet by donating to nonprofits like The Trustees, which focuses on local land conservation.

Contents

rice vinegar for tasty home meals 71

easy everyday ways to cook with amazake 93

simple and scrumptious dishes using shio koji 125

amazing natto recipes 149

introduction

Fermentation is deep-rooted in Japanese culture and an integral part of Japanese cooking. From drinks like amazake to seasonings like soy sauce, it's hard to find a Japanese dish that doesn't contain some sort of fermented ingredient. This is no surprise, since the most essential condiments used in Japanese cooking are miso, rice vinegar and soy sauce, which are all fermented. This is the true secret to Japanese cooking and what brings the delicious flavor to Japanese food.

Even when the main dish doesn't use fermented ingredients, in our home we usually eat pickled vegetables (tsukemono) or miso soup on the side. When I was growing up in Japan, my mother would always put a container of tsukemono on the table for everyone, no matter what dish we were eating. I grew up in a very small town called Hikigawa, where nearly all my family lived, so my mum would always ask me to pop over to my grandmother's place to pick up some of her homemade miso and tsukemono. Even now, my mother always makes her own tsukemono from daikon radishes that she harvests from her own garden.

I wish it was that simple now for Elizabeth and I to just run over and pick up some tsukemono and miso from my mother, but since moving to Australia, we've no longer had easy access to fermented ingredients. Since I grew up in Japan, and I've always cooked Japanese food for my children, my taste buds have been wired to a Japanese flavor, as have Elizabeth's. So it's always been essential for us to have fermented Japanese ingredients in the house to use every day. After we started our Japanese food blog, Chopstick Chronicles, we realized that these fermented ingredients are what bring flavor to our food and elevate every dish. I started to make fermented ingredients like miso at home, developed my own recipes and learned to cook many things at home for myself and my family.

I especially love to use fermented food in my cooking because of how beneficial it is to the body. Fermentation first started as a method to preserve food. The process of fermentation involves natural bacteria converting sugars and starches into alcohol or lactic acids, which preserves the nutrients in the food, breaks it down into a more digestible form and creates probiotics, enzymes, B vitamins and omega-3 fatty acids. By eating fermented foods, the beneficial probiotic bacteria and enzymes aid in increasing your digestive and immune systems and improving your overall health. This may be why the Japanese diet is considered so healthy and a contributing factor to the longevity of Japanese people. As the benefits of probiotic bacteria have become well known, a multitude of probiotic supplements have hit the market and become popular; however, these can be of little benefit, because the bacteria can be damaged during the manufacturing, transport and storage processes. It is a much better idea to cook with natural fermented ingredients yourself and incorporate fermented foods into your diet.

The recipes within this book will help you bring fermented food into your life through simple and flavorful everyday Japanese dishes. From main meals to drinks to desserts, there are endless ways for you to use fermented ingredients to bring the power of umami flavor into your meals and increase the healthiness of every dish.

Shihoko Ura   Elizabeth McClelland

delicious home-cooked dishes with *Miso*

Miso is one of the most commonly used and well-known fermented foods from Japan. I use it in so many dishes because it's one of my favorite flavors, and perfect for marinating meats and cooking with vegetables.

Miso can be classified by the color (red, white or mixed) or by the ingredient used (rice, barley or beans). There are two main types of miso, red (aka) and white (shiro). They both use the same basic ingredients but differ in taste and color due to the length of their fermentation process. The longer it is fermented, the darker the miso. The flavor can range from salty to sweet, which is why miso is such a versatile fermented food and an easy ingredient to use when cooking. For every recipe in this chapter you can change the color of the miso depending on how mild or strong you want the flavor to be. White miso will give the recipe a sweet, mild and subtle miso flavor, whereas red miso will be stronger and saltier.

I do like to make my own miso whenever I can. While the process of making miso is long, it is also very easy and rewarding. Otherwise, I use store-bought when I'm in a hurry.

Miso is an important ingredient in Japanese cuisine and adds a unique and delicious flavor to a variety of dishes from Miso Ground Pork Spring Rolls (page 54) to Chicken Miso Teriyaki (page 45) to desserts like Perfectly Creamy No-Churn Miso Ice Cream (page 66) and Classic Crème Brûlée with a Touch of Miso (page 58). This chapter will show you the many ways you can use miso in your cooking!

basic homemade miso

Making your own miso is not difficult and though it's a long process, it's all worthwhile in the end. You can tailor the recipe to your tastes to truly make it your own and worthy to pass down to the next generation. This recipe will make whatever color miso you like. I usually make white miso, but you can leave your miso to ferment for over six months if you want red miso. It's really up to you!

yield: 4 cups (1 L)
fermentation time: 3 to 6 months

1 cup (200 g) soybeans

7 tbsp (130 g) salt, plus 2 tbsp (35 g) for topping

16 oz (454 g) rice koji

½ cup (120 ml) reserved cooking water from soybeans

Wash the soybeans under running water. Soak the washed soybeans for 18 to 24 hours, then drain the water and place them in a pressure cooker. Add enough water to cover the soybeans, lock the lid in place and set the timer to pressure-cook for 10 minutes. When the 10 minutes are up, let the pressure come down naturally. If you don't have a pressure cooker you can cook the beans in a regular pot; allow the beans to simmer in the pot for 7 hours. While the soybeans are being cooked, place 7 tablespoons (130 g) of salt and the koji in a mixing bowl, mix and set aside. Pick one bean out of the pot and see if you can squish it with your fingertips. If it can be squished, it is the right softness to mash.

Mash the cooked soybeans with a potato masher or a mixer with a mincer attachment. Reserve the soybean cooking water, place the mashed soybeans in a large mixing bowl while they are still hot and add the salt and koji mixture to the bowl. Mix well with your hands until a coarse, but soft texture is reached, then add ¼ to ½ cup (60 to 120 ml) of the reserved soybean cooking water, if necessary.

Form the mashed soybeans into eight baseball-sized balls. Place the soybean balls into a container that is going to be used for the fermenting. Press the balls into the container tightly to force any air bubbles out, repeating the process until all the soybean balls are pressed into the container. Smooth the surface and wipe off any soybean mash from the container, then sprinkle salt to cover. Add 2 tablespoons (35 g) of salt to a ziplock bag and seal. Place the bag on top of the soybean balls, then cover the container with cling wrap and place the lid on top. Write the date prepared on the lid, then store the container in a dark and cool place for at least 3 months.

After 3 months, open the lid, remove the ziplock bag and turn the mixture with a wooden spatula. The miso should be white, so you can transfer it to the fridge until you are ready to use it. However, if you want red miso, then after the 3 months, smooth the surface of the miso again and place cling wrap on top. Place the container back in a dark and cool place for another 2 to 3 months. After 2 to 3 months, transfer the container to the fridge in order to stop the miso from over-fermenting. Due to its salt content, the miso will keep in the fridge for a long time without going bad.

root vegetable miso soup

Adding root vegetables will make classic miso soup heartier and more comforting. You can use whatever type of miso you like depending on your personal preference; white miso is subtler while red miso will give the soup a stronger flavor. Whenever you make miso soup, don't let it boil! Otherwise you will lose the miso flavor.

yield: 2 servings

1 medium onion

2 tsp (10 g) butter

¼ lb (100 g) pork belly, thinly sliced

¾ cup (100 g) diced sweet potato

¼ cup (30 g) diced carrots

⅓ cup (40 g) diced daikon radish

¼ cup (30 g) lotus root (renkon), sliced

1¼ cups (300 ml) water

1½ tbsp (24 g) Basic Homemade Miso (page 10)

Finely chopped scallions, for garnish

Cut the onion in half and then into wedges and set aside.

Heat the butter in a small saucepan over medium heat. When the butter has melted, add the pork and cook for 2 minutes. Add the diced sweet potato, carrots, daikon radish, lotus root and onion to the saucepan. Stir to coat the vegetables with the butter. Add the water to the pan and bring it to a simmer. Simmer for 5 minutes, until the vegetables are cooked, then remove the pan from the heat. Add the miso to the soup and stir to dissolve the paste into the stock, then put the saucepan back on the burner at medium heat. Turn the heat off just before it boils. Serve immediately in a small soup bowl and garnish with scallions.

miso-glazed tofu

This is one of the go-to recipes that my daughter Elizabeth and I both love to cook. It's so quick and simple but also tasty and nutritious. The miso glaze gives a delicious flavor to basic tofu.

yield: 2 servings

7 oz (200 g) firm tofu

3 tbsp (48 g) Basic Homemade Miso (page 10)

3 tbsp (45 g) sugar

1 tbsp (15 ml) mirin rice wine

1 tbsp (15 ml) sake

½ tbsp (7 g) grated ginger root, for garnish

¼ tsp white sesame seeds, for garnish

Wrap the tofu in a paper towel and place it on a small cutting board. Put something heavy like a flat plate over the wrapped tofu and lift one end of the cutting board up slightly in order to drain the excess water out of the tofu. Set it aside for 20 minutes.

While the excess water is being drained from the tofu, make the miso glaze. Mix together the miso and sugar. Add the mirin and sake, mixing well after each addition.

Preheat the oven to 350°F (180°C) on the broil (grill) setting. Cut the tofu into 1 x 1–inch (3 x 3–cm) squares, ½ inch (1 cm) thick, and skewer two pieces onto each skewer.

Lightly spray a frying pan with olive oil spray. Place the pan over medium heat and add the skewered tofu pieces. Fry one side for 2 minutes over medium heat until brown. Flip the pieces and brown the other side for 2 minutes. Line a baking tray with parchment paper and place the tofu skewers on the tray. Brush the miso glaze over the tofu. Broil (grill) for a few minutes in the preheated oven. Place the skewers on a flat plate and garnish with the grated ginger. Sprinkle the white sesame seeds on top of each tofu skewer.

miso tofu dip two ways

Veggie sticks or crackers with dip is my favorite healthy snack, and if the dip has a fermented ingredient, even better! This dip is super quick and easy and can be made sweet or savory so it'll suit any taste buds.

yield: 2 small bowls

sweet miso dip

2 tbsp (30 g) white Basic Homemade Miso (page 10)

3 tbsp (50 g) firm tofu

2 tbsp (30 g) unsalted natural peanut butter

2 tbsp (30 ml) honey

White sesame seeds, for garnish

savory miso dip

2 tbsp (30 g) red Basic Homemade Miso (page 10)

3 tbsp (50 g) firm tofu

½ tbsp (4 g) grated garlic

Pine nuts, for garnish

Crackers, for serving
Raw vegetables, chopped, for serving

For the sweet miso dip, place the white miso, firm tofu, peanut butter and honey in a food processor and blitz for 30 seconds. If you don't have a food processor, you can mix all the ingredients using a mortar and pestle. Garnish with white sesame seeds.

For the savory miso dip, place the red miso, tofu and garlic in a food processor and blitz for 30 seconds. Garnish with pine nuts.

Serve the dip in a bowl with crackers or raw chopped vegetables such as celery, cucumber and carrots. Store the dip in an airtight container and it will keep for a couple days in the fridge.

succulent scallops glazed with miso

This is a very delicate and simple looking dish, but the taste is anything but modest. The subtle touch of white miso goes so well with the scallops and always leaves my guests wanting more when I serve this dish as an appetizer.

yield: 2 servings

2 tsp (10 ml) sake

8 scallops

1 tbsp (15 g) white Basic Homemade Miso (page 10)

1 tsp mirin

1 tsp honey

1 tbsp (15 g) butter

Sprinkle the sake over the scallops and let them rest for 5 minutes. Combine the miso, mirin and honey in a small bowl and set aside.

Preheat the oven to 350°F (180°C) on the broil (grill) setting.

Heat the butter in a frying pan over medium heat. Pat the scallops dry with a paper towel and pan-fry for 2 minutes on each side. Glaze the top of the scallops with the miso mixture and put them into the oven. I put my whole frying pan into the oven, but if you don't have an ovenproof frying pan you can transfer them to a baking tray lined with parchment paper. Let them broil (grill) in the oven for 5 minutes.

simmered daikon radish dressed with sweet miso

You can eat these both hot and cold, so they're perfect for any season. I like to make a few batches at a time and save them in the fridge for days when I need a light dinner, don't have time to cook or when I want to add some extra veggies to a meal.

yield: 2 servings

1 lb (454 g) daikon radish

1 tbsp (15 g) short-grain Japanese koshihikari rice

6 cups (1.5 L) water, divided

1 tsp soy sauce

1 tbsp (15 ml) sake

2-inch (5-cm) dried kelp strip (kombu)

miso dressing

2 tbsp (30 g) Basic Homemade Miso (page 10)

1 tbsp (15 ml) mirin

2 tbsp (30 g) sugar

1 tbsp (15 ml) sake

White sesame seeds, for garnish

Cut the daikon into pieces about 1 inch (3 cm) thick. Use a knife or grater to shave the edges of the daikon pieces. Score the top of each piece of daikon so that the seasoning and flavor will absorb.

You won't actually eat the rice in this recipe, but it is essential to add because it absorbs the film and the acidity created when boiling the daikon. I place the rice into an empty tea bag first, which makes it easier to remove later, but if you don't have them it's okay to add the loose rice.

In a large pot, place 3 cups (710 ml) of water and add the daikon and rice. Simmer the daikon and rice over low heat for 30 minutes. Remove it from the heat, drain the water and remove the rice. Add another 3 cups (710 ml) of water to the daikon in the pot and add the soy sauce, sake and kelp strip. Bring it to a boil, then turn the heat to low and allow it to simmer for 40 minutes.

While the daikon is simmering, stir together the miso, mirin, sugar and sake in a small saucepan. Cook it over low heat until the sauce thickens, for about 5 minutes. When the daikon is soft enough for a skewer to easily go through, remove the kelp strip from the pot and discard. Remove the daikon pieces from the heat and place them in a small bowl. Top with the miso dressing and sprinkle some sesame seeds on top.

note: If possible, use the middle or root end of the daikon because the ends are more bitter.

creamy miso prawn stew

This soup is the perfect balance of miso and prawns. Eat it with some buttered toast and you'll be scraping every last bit of stew out of the bowl!

yield: 4 servings

12 tiger prawns

1 tbsp (15 g) butter

½ cup (120 ml) water

1 tbsp (15 ml) olive oil

⅓ cup (42 g) carrots, diced

2 oz (50 g) frozen lotus roots (renkon), sliced

¾ cup (110 g) potato, diced

⅓ cup (50 g) onion, diced

2 tbsp (30 g) white Basic Homemade Miso (page 10)

1 serving of White Sauce (page 168)

1¼ cups (50 g) broccolini, chopped

Salt and pepper, to taste

Remove the shells from the prawns, devein and clean them. Keep the shells and heads of the prawns to use for the stock.

Heat the butter in a saucepan over medium heat and add the prawn shells and heads. Cook until the shells and heads change color, about 3 minutes. Once the shells and heads change color, add the water and bring it to boil. Remove the stock from the heat and discard the prawn shells and heads.

Heat the olive oil in a large pot over medium heat and add the carrots, lotus roots, potato and onion. Stir-fry the vegetables for 5 minutes or until the edges of the potatoes become slightly transparent and the vegetables are coated well with the oil, then add the prawns and the prawn stock. Bring the stew to a boil, then lower the heat and simmer for 15 minutes. Add the miso to the pot and stir to dissolve it. Add the white sauce and stir thoroughly. Add the broccolini and continue to cook the stew for 3 more minutes, until the broccolini is cooked. Remove it from the heat and season with salt and pepper to taste.

note: Make sure not to use banana prawns because the prawn flavor will be too overpowering. Tiger prawns work much better in this recipe.

grilled miso-glazed rice balls

Rice balls, called onigiri or omusubi in Japanese, are a super common Japanese food. You'll find them almost anywhere and with many different types of fillings. I like to glaze my onigiri with miso because it goes so well with the plain white rice. The rice can be formed into balls, but a triangular shape adds a fun twist to this dish. It takes a bit of practice to get the hang of making the rice into a triangular shape, but it's not hard to master, so hang in there!

yield: 6 rice balls

rice balls

2 cups (400 g) uncooked short-grain Japanese koshihikari rice

1 tbsp (15 ml) sesame oil

miso glaze

1 tbsp (15 g) red Basic Homemade Miso (page 10)

1 tbsp (15 ml) sake

1 tbsp (15 g) sugar

1 tbsp (15 g) white sesame seeds, for garnish

2 tbsp (30 g) chopped scallions, for garnish

Cook the rice in your rice cooker or in a pot. Make sure you use Japanese-style sushi rice because it is stickier and the onigiri will be able to come together properly. Once the rice is cooked, lay down some cling wrap and scoop ⅙ of the rice onto the cling wrap. Wrap the cling wrap over the rice and squish the rice with your hands to form it into a round or triangular shape. Repeat this process with the remaining rice to make six onigiri in total, then remove the cling wrap and set them aside.

For the glaze, mix the red miso, sake and sugar together in a small bowl. Coat each onigiri with the glaze. I use a pastry brush to do this; it makes it a lot easier.

Heat some sesame oil in a frying pan and fry the onigiri for 2 minutes on each side over medium heat. Remove it from the heat and sprinkle it with the sesame seeds and scallions to garnish.

rice gratin with white miso sauce

Rice gratin (we call it doria in Japan) is such a tasty comfort food. The creamy white sauce with melted cheese over rice is complemented nicely with the white miso, adding an extra pack of flavor.

yield: 2 servings

2 tsp (10 g) butter

⅓ cup (42 g) diced carrot

⅓ cup (50 g) finely chopped onion

3 cups (600 g) cooked short-grain Japanese koshihikari rice

1 tbsp (15 ml) olive oil

4 oz (100 g) chicken breast, cut into bite-size chunks

1 cup (100 g) shimeji mushrooms (or regular white mushrooms)

1½ servings White Sauce (page 168)

1 tbsp (15 g) white Basic Homemade Miso (page 10)

½ cup (60 g) grated cheddar or mozzarella cheese

Salt and pepper, to taste

1 tsp chopped parsley, for garnish

Preheat the oven to 400°F (200°C). Heat the butter in a large frying pan on medium heat and cook the carrot and onion until soft, 3 to 5 minutes. Add the cooked rice and stir them together, then remove the pan from the heat and set it aside.

In another frying pan, heat the oil and cook the chopped chicken and mushrooms on medium heat until the chicken is cooked all the way through, 5 to 7 minutes. Add the white sauce and miso to the frying pan with the chicken and mushrooms, mix them together, then remove it from the heat and set aside.

Divide the rice mixture into two small oven dishes. Top the rice with the chicken and white sauce mixture and sprinkle some cheese over the top. Cook it in the oven until the cheese is browned. Remove it from the oven, and season with salt and pepper to taste and garnish with chopped parsley.

note: Shimeji mushrooms are used often in Japanese cooking. They are small with long stems and can be found in most Asian grocery stores.

simple miso rice porridge

In Japan, this is called zousui. It is basically steamed rice simmered in miso soup and is most often cooked with vegetables and egg. Whenever Elizabeth or I have a cold or feel the need for a thick, comforting soup to eat during winter, I make this porridge for us.

yield: 2 servings

1⅓ cups (270 g) cooked short-grain Japanese koshihikari rice

1¾ cups (420 ml) Dashi with Bonito Flakes and Kelp (page 168)

2 tbsp (30 g) red Basic Homemade Miso (page 10)

2 eggs

1 tbsp (15 g) finely chopped scallions

Place the rice and dashi stock into a saucepan and bring it to a boil. Once it boils, turn the heat to low. Add the miso to the saucepan and let it dissolve. Stir it well.

Crack the eggs in a separate small bowl and lightly whisk. Add the eggs to the saucepan but don't stir it right away. If you mix it right away, the egg won't have a chance to cook and form and it will just mix in with everything. Leave it to sit for 1 minute, then gently mix it into the rice. Sprinkle the chopped scallions into the pan and remove it from the heat.

miso cream pasta

This is a Japanese twist on a creamy pasta dish. The bacon, mushrooms and miso create this powerful and wonderful flavor combination that goes so well with the creaminess of the pasta. Since it's so easy to prepare, I like to make it on weeknights when I don't have as much time to cook.

yield: 2 servings

6 oz (170 g) spaghetti

2 tsp (10 g) butter

4 oz (100 g) chopped bacon

⅓ cup (50 g) finely chopped onion

1 cup (100 g) shimeji mushrooms, trimmed

2 oz (50 ml) heavy cream

7 oz (200 ml) milk

1 tbsp (15 g) white Basic Homemade Miso (page 10)

Salt and pepper, to taste

Grated Parmesan cheese, for garnish

Boil a pot of water with a pinch of salt to cook the spaghetti al dente, according to package directions. Drain the water and set the pasta aside.

Heat the butter in a frying pan over medium heat and cook the bacon and onion until they are thoroughly cooked and browned, 5 minutes. Add the shimeji mushrooms and cook until the mushrooms are soft, 2 to 3 minutes. Add the cream and milk to the pan and stir. Once it starts to bubble, add the miso and stir to mix it in well. Add salt and pepper to taste. Add the cooked pasta and stir well to coat it with the sauce. Remove the pan from the heat and serve with grated Parmesan cheese.

japanese-style mabo tofu

Mabo tofu is a very popular Chinese dish in Japan. It's one of my go-to healthy dishes because it's packed full of protein from the meat and tofu, and I can make a large batch of it for the week. The Chinese version doesn't use miso, but in Japan we use it to add our favorite umami flavor and suit our tastes. The subtle spiciness of the dish goes perfectly with plain steamed rice. This is Elizabeth's favorite Japanese dish to cook because it's so easy but still has that comforting Japanese flavor.

yield: 4 servings

12 oz (340 g) firm tofu

1 tsp tobanjan chili paste

2 tbsp (30 ml) sake

1 tbsp (15 g) red Basic Homemade Miso (page 10)

1 tbsp (15 ml) soy sauce

½ tbsp (7 g) sugar

½ tbsp (7 ml) sesame oil

1 clove garlic, minced

1 tsp minced ginger root

2 tbsp (15 g) chopped scallions

1 lb (454 g) ground beef

1 tsp torigara soup mixed with 1 cup (250 ml) water

1 tbsp (15 g) potato starch (katakuriko)

1 tbsp (15 ml) water

Steamed rice, to serve

First, drain the water from the tofu by covering it with a paper towel and microwaving it for 2 minutes. Alternatively, you can cover the tofu with a paper towel, put it on a wire rack and put a plate on top for 30 minutes. Then dice it into ¾-inch (2-cm) cubes.

Mix the tobanjan, sake, red miso, soy sauce and sugar together in a small bowl and set it aside.

Heat the sesame seed oil in a large frying pan over medium heat and add the garlic, ginger and scallions. When it becomes fragrant, add the ground beef and cook until it has changed color. Add the sauce and stir it together, then add the torigara soup (diluted with the water) and when it starts to boil, add the tofu. Leave it to cook for a few minutes on medium heat—don't stir right away because the tofu will break. Once the tofu has cooked and hardened a bit, stir it gently.

In a small bowl, add the potato starch and mix it with the water. Slightly tilt the frying pan and add the potato starch to the liquid that piles to one side. Stir it gently, then put the frying pan back flat on the burner and stir it all together. Remove it from the heat and serve with plain steamed rice.

notes: Torigara soup means "chicken carcass soup." It is a soup stock powder similar to chicken stock, which we add to various recipes to bring more flavor. You can buy it in packets in Japan or make it at home yourself with a chicken carcass.

Katakuriko is potato starch. It is used as a thickener when cooking and as a coating when deep-frying foods. You can usually buy it online or in Asian/Japanese stores, but if you really can't find it you can substitute with cornstarch.

green beans dressed with sesame miso

This mildly sweet and salty dish is an easy and healthy addition to any meal. It's great as a side dish, and I also like to add this to my bento boxes for lunch. If you prefer, you can get a store-bought version of the mixed miso (awase miso) for this recipe, or use the recipe in this book to make your own Basic Homemade Miso (page 10). This recipe is perfect for people who aren't so keen on vegetables because the miso makes it taste so delicious.

yield: 2 servings

1 cup (120 g) green beans

5 tbsp (45 g) white sesame seeds

2 tbsp (30 g) mixed red and white Basic Homemade Miso (page 10)

2 tbsp (30 g) sugar

1 tsp soy sauce

Trim the edges of the green beans and parboil them in a pot of water with a pinch of salt. Drain the water and set the beans aside.

In a mortar or bowl, grind the sesame seeds and set them aside. In a small saucepan, add the miso, sugar and soy sauce and keep stirring it over medium heat until it becomes glossy. Remove the sauce from the heat, add it to the mortar with the sesame seeds and grind it all together. Chop the green beans into 1¼-inch (3-cm) pieces and add them to the mortar. Coat well with the sesame mixture and serve.

pork and cabbage miso stir-fry

Miso is often mixed with other condiments such as soy sauce and sugar to season and add flavor, like this miso stir-fry. Miso adds the richness of umami and enhances the overall flavor of the meat and vegetables.

yield: 2 servings

⅔ lb (300 g) pork belly

2 tbsp (30 g) red Basic Homemade Miso (page 10)

¼ tsp tobanjan

1 tbsp (15 g) sugar

2 tbsp (30 ml) sake

1 tsp soy sauce

4 tbsp (40 g) potato starch (katakuriko)

¼ head green cabbage, roughly torn

¾ cup (110 g) chopped capsicum/ bell pepper

½ cup (60 g) chopped celery

1 tbsp (15 ml) olive oil

2 tbsp (30 g) finely chopped scallions

1 clove garlic, minced

Steamed rice, to serve

Slice the pork belly thinly. I usually buy mine already sliced from Japanese grocery stores or ask a butcher to slice it thin. If you can't get presliced pork, it is easier to slice the meat thinly when it is semi-frozen.

To make the sauce, combine the miso, tobanjan, sugar, sake and soy sauce in a mortar or bowl and set aside.

Dust the potato starch on the pork and coat the meat evenly. I usually put the meat and the potato starch in a large ziplock bag and shake it to dust and coat evenly.

Boil water in a large pot and parboil the cabbage, bell pepper and celery for 1 minute. Drain the water and set the vegetables aside.

Heat the olive oil in a frying pan over high heat and cook the pork until it is browned, 3 to 5 minutes. Move the pork to the side of the frying pan and add the scallions and the minced garlic. When the garlic and scallions are fragrant, add the miso sauce mixture to the frying pan. When the sauce mixture is fragrant, stir everything together to coat the pork with the sauce. Add the parboiled vegetables and toss it all together. Turn the heat off once it is all stir-fried. Serve with plain steamed rice.

note: Tobanjan is a spicy Sichuan-style paste made from fermented beans. We use it often in Japanese cooking when making mabo tofu and other dishes needing spice. You can buy it in Asian/Japanese grocery stores and online.

miso udon stew

This was one of my monthly treat meals when I worked as a nurse in Japan. The other nurses and I would all request a day off to go eat this together because it's so tasty, and the warm, steamy stew made us feel so relaxed. Now I like to make it at home and it always brings back those memories.

yield: 2 servings

1 piece fried tofu (age tofu)

2 (6-oz [170-g]) packages udon noodles

0.7 qt (660 ml) Dashi with Bonito Flakes and Kelp (page 168)

2 tbsp (30 g) red Basic Homemade Miso (page 10)

1 tbsp (15 ml) sake

½ tbsp (7 g) sugar

1 chicken thigh, chopped into bite-size pieces

2 shiitake mushrooms, chopped in half, stalk discarded

4 pieces Naruto fish cakes

1 stalk scallions, finely chopped, for garnish

Seven-spice chili powder (shichimi togarashi), for garnish, optional

Prepare the fried tofu by putting it in a sieve or holding it with chopsticks or tongs, then pouring boiling water over it to remove the excess oil. Once it's cooled down, squeeze out more of the water. Cut it into small strips and set it aside.

If you are using frozen udon noodles, defrost them by pouring boiling water over them in a pot then draining out the water.

In a hot pot or large pot, add the dashi stock and bring it to a boil. Reduce the heat and add the miso, sake and sugar, and mix it together to make the soup. Add the chicken and mushrooms and cook for 2 minutes. Add the udon, fish cakes and fried tofu and cook for 2 minutes. Remove the stew from the heat and garnish with the scallions and chili powder, if using.

note: Naruto is a cured fish surimi (paste), with a pink spiral in the center. It is available at Asian or Japanese supermarkets, but can be left out of this recipe if you cannot find it.

ultimate miso ramen

There are many different types of ramen, such as the pork bone (tonkotsu) and soy sauce varieties. My favorite ramen base is miso ramen because I just really love the flavor. If you have the time, you can make the broth from scratch, but an easy shortcut is to just use an instant ramen soup—which is what most Japanese people use. You can also use torigara soup (see note on page 33), which is a type of chicken stock used in some of the other recipes in this book.

yield: 2 servings

2½ cups (600 ml) water, plus more for boiling

1 tbsp (15 ml) torigara soup

½ tsp salt

1 tbsp (15 ml) sake

1 cup (100 g) bean sprouts

3 tbsp (30 g) corn kernels, canned or frozen

2 tsp (10 g) butter

2 tbsp (30 g) red Basic Homemade Miso (page 10)

2 packets ramen noodles

2 boiled eggs

1 tbsp (15 g) finely chopped scallions

2 slices char siu pork

Start to boil some water in a large pot. In another pot, add the 2½ cups (600 ml) of water, the torigara soup, salt and sake. Mix well and leave it to simmer on low heat while the other pot of water continues to get to a boiling point.

In the meantime, toss the bean sprouts and corn in a frying pan with the butter for about 3 minutes and set it aside. Now prepare the bowls of ramen by putting 1 tablespoon (15 g) of miso each into two bowls. Remove the soup from the heat and divide it equally into the bowls. Set them aside.

The large pot of water should now be boiling; add the ramen noodles and cook for 1 minute. Remove the pot from the heat and drain the noodles using a sieve or a colander. Divide the noodles equally into the two bowls with the soup. Divide the bean sprouts, corn, eggs, scallions and pork equally on top of the noodles. Serve immediately.

note: Char siu pork is pork belly rolled up and simmered for a long time in a soy sauce–based broth. If you can't find char siu pork, you can make it yourself or use bacon.

ginger-miso pork with scallions

Ginger pork (shoga yaki) is a common pork dish in Japan. Adding miso gives it an extra umami flavor to make it burst with deliciousness. This goes perfectly with plain steamed rice.

yield: 2 servings

sauce

½ tbsp (7 ml) ginger juice

1 tbsp (15 ml) soy sauce

1 tbsp (15 ml) sake

1 tbsp (15 ml) mirin

1 tbsp (15 g) red Basic Homemade Miso (page 10)

½ lb (227 g) pork loin, thinly sliced

½ tsp salt

2 tsp (10 ml) sake

1 tbsp (8 g) cornstarch

Sesame or vegetable oil, for frying

1 tbsp (15 g) chopped scallions, for garnish

2 cups (140 g) thinly sliced sugarloaf cabbage, to serve

To make the sauce, prepare the ginger juice by grating fresh ginger and squeezing out the juice. Combine the soy sauce, sake, mirin, red miso and ginger juice in a small bowl and set it aside.

Prepare the pork by making small cuts along the edge of the pork slices to avoid the pork curling up when it's cooked. Then sprinkle it with the salt, sake and cornstarch and dust off the excess.

Heat some oil in a frying pan and cook the pork until both sides are browned, for about 5 minutes in total. Pour the sauce over the pork and cook on high heat for 2 minutes, until the sauce has thickened and reduced a bit. Remove the pan from the heat and garnish with the scallions. Serve with the thinly sliced cabbage.

chicken miso teriyaki

Teriyaki chicken is one of the most well-known Japanese foods and something that I cook frequently because it's so simple. Sometimes I like to add miso to give it a bit of a twist.

yield: 2 servings

sauce

½ tsp torigara soup powder

1 tbsp (15 ml) sake

1 tbsp (15 g) sugar

2 tbsp (30 g) red Basic Homemade Miso (page 10)

3 tbsp (45 ml) water

2 chicken thighs, skinless and boneless

½ tbsp (7 g) sesame oil

½ tsp sesame seeds, for garnish

1 tsp finely chopped scallions, for garnish

Prepare the sauce by mixing together the torigara soup powder, sake, sugar, red miso and water. Set it aside.

Cut the chicken thighs into small bite-size pieces. Heat the sesame oil in a frying pan on high heat. Once the pan has heated, add the chicken. Cook until the skin is browned and crispy, 3 to 5 minutes, then turn the chicken over and cook the other side until it is browned. Pour the sauce over the chicken and keep coating the chicken with the sauce on high heat for 2 minutes, until it thickens and reduces a bit. Once it has thickened, remove the pan from the heat and garnish the chicken with sesame seeds and scallions before serving.

miso beef bowl

This beef bowl (gyudon) is like Japanese fast food; it's easy to make and very filling. Some people eat it with a raw egg, but I prefer to cook the egg a bit with the beef before serving it.

yield: 2 servings

½ cup (120 ml) Dashi with Bonito Flakes and Kelp (page 168)

1 tbsp (15 ml) sake

1 tbsp (15 g) red Basic Homemade Miso (page 10)

½ tbsp (7 ml) mirin

½ tbsp (7 ml) soy sauce

1 tbsp (15 g) sugar

½ onion, sliced

⅓ lb (150 g) sirloin beef, thinly sliced

2 eggs

3 cups (600 g) cooked short-grain Japanese koshihikari rice

Seven-spice chili powder (shichimi togarashi), to taste

In a shallow saucepan or a frying pan, place the dashi, sake, miso, mirin, soy sauce and sugar. Mix them together and bring it to a boil.

Once it boils, turn the heat down to medium and add the onion and beef. Cook for about 5 minutes. With a little ladle or sieve, remove the foam that accumulates on the top. During the last 2 minutes of cooking, crack both eggs into the pot and allow them to cook to your desired doneness, at least halfway.

Divide the rice into two bowls, then remove the pot from the heat and divide the beef mixture into the bowls. Sprinkle chili powder to taste.

easy miso ground pork

(nikumiso)

This is a Japanese staple ingredient that can be used in many different dishes. In Japan, we call it tsukuri oki, which basically means "cook and leave." We make a large amount and leave it in the fridge to use in different dishes and for bento boxes throughout the week.

yield: 1 lb (454 g)

1½ tbsp (22 ml) sesame oil

1 clove of garlic, minced

1 tbsp (15 g) grated ginger root

1¼ cups (200 g) finely chopped onion

1 lb (454 g) ground pork

2 tbsp (30 ml) sake

½ cup (120 ml) water

3 tbsp (45 g) red Basic Homemade Miso (page 10)

3 tbsp (45 g) white sugar

Heat the sesame oil in a large frying pan over medium heat. Add the garlic and ginger. When it becomes fragrant, add the onion and cook until it is soft. Once the onion is soft, add the ground pork and cook until the meat is no longer pink.

Combine the sake, water, miso and sugar in a small bowl, then pour it over the meat in the frying pan. Stir it together and cook (stirring occasionally) until the liquid has evaporated and absorbed into the pork. Remove from the heat and keep it in the fridge in an airtight container for a week, or in the freezer for up to a month.

fresh lettuce wraps with miso ground pork

This is one of the quickest and easiest recipes to use leftover Easy Miso Ground Pork (page 49). It's a real party pleaser because you can just place all the ingredients on a table and everyone can grab a lettuce wrap and top it with whatever they like (of course, the ground pork is a must!).

yield: 6 lettuce wraps

⅓ lb (150 g) Easy Miso Ground Pork (page 49)

½ cup (60 g) bean sprouts

½ cup (60 g) grated carrot

6 shiso leaves, optional

6 iceberg lettuce leaves

Sesame seeds, for garnish

Place a bit of the pork, bean sprouts, carrot and shiso leaves into the lettuce cups and sprinkle with sesame seeds. Done!

note: Shiso is a variety of plant of the genus *Perilla*. It comes in both a green and purple variety and both are used extensively in Japanese cooking. It has a unique flavor and brings a distinct and strong taste to dishes. I love to use it whenever I can and grow my own shiso plant because it's not the easiest to find at grocery stores and markets.

miso ground pork udon

This is another way you can use any leftover Easy Miso Ground Pork (page 49). The flavor of the pork goes so well with the udon noodles.

yield: 2 servings

soup

2 tbsp (30 ml) soy sauce

2 tbsp (30 ml) mirin

2 tbsp (30 ml) Dashi with Bonito Flakes and Kelp (page 168)

2 (6-oz [170-g]) packages udon noodles

¼ lb (100 g) Easy Miso Ground Pork (page 49)

2 tbsp (30 g) chopped scallions

A pinch of seven-spice chili powder (shichimi togarashi), for garnish

To make the soup, place the soy sauce, mirin and dashi in a small saucepan and bring it to a boil. Remove it from the heat and set it aside.

Put enough water in a pot to cook the udon noodles and bring it to a boil. Once the water boils, add the udon noodles and cook for 2 minutes. Drain the water and divide the noodles into two bowls.

Divide the pork into the two bowls of noodles and garnish with the scallions. Use a ladle to pour the soup equally into the bowls. Sprinkle it with the chili powder to garnish.

miso ground pork spring rolls

This is my favorite way to use leftover nikumiso because I really love spring rolls. They are fun to roll up and they taste delicious. I always serve them with sweet chili sauce.

yield: 10 spring rolls

10 (6 x 6–in [15 x 15–cm]) spring roll sheets

¼ lb (100 g) Easy Miso Ground Pork (page 49), divided

⅔ cup (70 g) bean sprouts, divided

⅓ cup (42 g) grated carrot, divided

2 cups (500 ml) sesame or vegetable oil, for frying

Sweet chili sauce, to serve

Place 1 spring roll sheet diagonally in front of you on a counter or table. Put 1½ tablespoons (22 g) of pork in the center of the sheet and press it out into a small cylinder shape. Add about 2 teaspoons (5 g) of bean sprouts and about 1 teaspoon of grated carrot and lay them out next to the meat.

Pinch the corner closest to yourself, fold it over the fillings and roll it tightly. Fold the left and right side into the center of the spring roll and roll it once tightly. Dip your finger in a bit of water and press the last end corner with the water. Tightly roll the spring roll to the end and seal it with the water you pressed onto the corner. Repeat this process for the remaining spring rolls.

Use a deep fryer or fill a deep pan or wok with the oil. Once the oil has heated to about 350°F (180°C) and has some little bubbles, add five spring rolls at a time to the pan. Once they look golden and crispy, 5 minutes, remove them from the oil and lay them on a tray or plate lined with a paper towel. Repeat the process with the remaining rolls. Serve them with sweet chili sauce.

miso sukiyaki

Sukiyaki is a Japanese hot pot dish (nabemono) made with vegetables, meat and tofu. The dish as a whole has a semisweet flavor, but everything within sukiyaki has a different taste, so you can pick whatever you like out of the pot—"sukiyaki" basically means "cook what you like." It's the perfect thing to make in the colder months and a lovely family meal because everyone can cook together at the table. This is what Elizabeth and I do with our family every time we go back to Japan at Christmastime.

yield: 4 servings

broth

2 cups (500 ml) Dashi with Bonito Flakes and Kelp (page 168)

5 tbsp (75 g) red Basic Homemade Miso (page 10)

3 tbsp (45 ml) sake

3 tbsp (45 ml) mirin

3 tbsp (45 ml) soy sauce

3 tbsp (45 g) sugar

1 tbsp (15 ml) sesame or vegetable oil, or 1 small cube of lard

¾ lb (340 g) sirloin beef, thinly sliced, divided

½ bunch scallions, cut into large slices, divided

½ medium-sized Chinese (Napa) cabbage, chopped into large chunks, divided

12 oz (340 g) tofu, largely cubed, divided

1 bunch shimeji mushrooms, divided

To prepare the broth, add the dashi, miso, sake, mirin, soy sauce and sugar to a saucepan. Bring it to a boil, then remove it from the heat.

Heat a sukiyaki pan (hot pot pan) or a cast-iron frying pan on medium heat on a portable stove set on the dining table. Heat the oil or lard in the pan and cook half of the meat. Once the meat changes color, add half of the scallions and half of the cabbage. Add half of the tofu and half of the mushrooms, then add half of the broth and let the vegetables simmer in the sauce. Once everything starts to cook, start to eat straight from the pot, and keep adding the rest of the ingredients as you eat and as you like.

note: In Japan, people crack and whisk an egg in its own little bowl and use it as a dipping plate. However, if you would rather not eat raw eggs, you can add it to the hot pot to cook.

classic crème brûlée with a touch of miso

This is a classic French sweet infused with a touch of Japanese fermentation. I like to make a dessert like this when I have guests because it's easy to adjust the batch depending on how many people, and everyone gets their own little individual dessert.

yield: 4 servings

¾ cup (180 ml) heavy cream

¼ cup (60 ml) whole milk

2 tbsp (30 g) white Basic Homemade Miso (page 10)

4 egg yolks

3 tbsp (45 g) sugar, plus extra for topping

Preheat the oven to 275°F (135°C). Combine the heavy cream and milk in a small bowl. Place the miso in a saucepan over low heat and add the cream and milk mixture a little bit at a time to dissolve the miso. Remove the mixture from the heat just before it boils. Let it cool until it is lukewarm.

Place the egg yolks and sugar in a mixing bowl and mix together. Add the lukewarm miso cream mixture into the egg yolks. Use a sieve to strain the mixture into another bowl to make it all smooth. Divide the crème brûlée equally into four ramekins.

Place the ramekins into a deep baking pan or casserole dish and pour enough water into the pan to come about halfway up the sides of the ramekins. Put the pan into the preheated oven and bake for 40 minutes.

After it's baked, remove the ramekins from the pan and refrigerate until they're set (overnight or for at least 6 to 7 hours). Once set, sprinkle the tops of the crème brûlées with sugar and use a small blowtorch to caramelize the sugar, or pop the ramekins in the oven on the broil (grill) setting until the top caramelizes.

sweet and salty miso brownies

The subtle saltiness of miso enriches the sweetness of baked goods and sweets. Adding a little bit of miso into chocolate brownies adds a delicious extra-salty flavor and gives it a bittersweet taste that will go perfectly with a warm cup of matcha tea.

yield: 9 brownies

½ cup (70 g) all-purpose flour

¼ cup (30 g) cocoa powder

3 eggs

¼ cup (30 g) crushed walnuts

¼ cup (50 g) unsalted butter

¼ cup (60 ml) heavy cream

2 oz (50 g) dark chocolate (I use Lindt 51% dark chocolate)

1 tbsp (15 g) white Basic Homemade Miso (page 10)

¼ tsp cream of tartar

½ cup (100 g) sugar, divided

Line a 12 x 12–inch (30 x 30–cm) cake tin with parchment paper. Preheat the oven to 350°F (180°C).

Sift the flour and cocoa powder together and set it aside. Separate the egg yolks and whites, set aside the yolks (do not mix them together), then pour the egg whites into a mixing bowl and refrigerate. Toast the walnuts in a small frying pan over low heat (as they are easily burned) for 2 to 3 minutes, shaking the frying pan constantly, then set them aside.

Create a double boiler to melt the chocolate. Fill a saucepan with water and heat until it reaches a simmer. Place the butter, cream, chocolate and miso in a heatproof bowl and set the bowl to float in the simmering pot. Stir the mixture continuously as it melts. When it has all melted and mixed well, remove the bowl from the saucepan. Add the egg yolks one at a time, stirring after each addition. Then set the bowl aside; it will cool down on its own while you make the meringue in a separate bowl.

To make the meringue, remove the egg whites from the refrigerator and add the cream of tartar to the bowl. Beat the egg whites until large bubbles form, then add a third of the sugar and continue beating. Repeat 2 more times with the remaining sugar and beat until the meringue is shiny and glossy with soft white peaks.

Add a third of the prepared meringue to the chocolate mixture and fold them together, being careful not to break the meringue. Repeat with another third of the meringue. Finally, pour the two-thirds of meringue and chocolate mixture into the meringue bowl and fold in the last of the meringue. Add the sifted flour and cocoa powder, being careful not to overmix. Add the toasted walnuts into the mixture. Pour the batter into the prepared cake tin. Bake it for 25 minutes. After 25 minutes, test the brownie by inserting a skewer. If it comes out clean, the brownie is done. Remove the tin from the oven and remove the brownie by pulling it out by the edges of the parchment paper. Cool the brownie on a cooling rack, then slice it as desired and serve.

umami miso-glazed apple tarte tatin

French desserts are popular in Japan and are often adapted to suit Japanese tastes. This one is a classic French apple tart made with miso, which gives the apples a very subtle saltiness. It's also quite easy; all you need is an ovenproof frying pan. You can serve this tarte tatin with some Perfectly Creamy No-Churn Miso Ice Cream (page 66) or some whipped cream.

yield: 1 tart

1 sheet puff pastry, thawed

1 tbsp (15 g) white Basic Homemade Miso (page 10)

1 tbsp (15 ml) water

⅓ cup (75 g) granulated or caster sugar

3 tbsp (40 g) butter, chopped

3 apples, peeled, cored and halved

Preheat the oven to 350°F (180°C). Measure your ovenproof frying pan (I use a cast-iron skillet) and cut out a circle in the puff pastry sheet to match that size. Instead of using 2 sheets of puff pastry, I just fold over the leftover corners of the pastry sheet to minimize waste and still make the pastry layer puffy and thick. Once you've done this, set it aside.

In the ovenproof frying pan over low heat, add the miso and water and stir it together with a wooden spoon to dissolve the miso. Add the sugar and stir them together until the sugar has dissolved. Once it has dissolved, turn the heat up to medium to bring it to a boil, then leave it (without stirring) until the sugar becomes golden brown, about 5 minutes. Add the butter to the pot carefully and melt it well into the sugar mixture. Turn the heat off and remove the pan from the heat.

Arrange the apple halves into the pan nicely with the cut side up, so when it is cooked and turned over, the nice round side will be up. Place the pastry sheet over the apples in the ovenproof frying pan and tuck the edges in. Bake for 40 minutes or until the pastry is puffed and golden brown. Turn off the oven, remove the tart and let it sit in the pan for 2 minutes. Place a serving plate over the frying pan and flip it over so the tart sits on the plate with the apples facing up. Cut and serve.

buttery miso-sesame cookies

Adding some white miso into cookies and other baked goods gives them a touch of salty flavor without being too overpowering, which I love. I like to enjoy these cookies with some Japanese tea or a nice Amazake Bubble Tea (page 117). Be sure to prepare these cookies in advance because you have to let the dough rise for 30 minutes.

yield: 40 cookies

1⅓ cups (165 g) all-purpose flour

¼ cup (30 g) almond meal

½ cup (100 g) unsalted butter, room temperature

½ cup (100 g) granulated or caster sugar

1 tbsp (15 g) white Basic Homemade Miso (page 10)

1 large egg

1 tbsp (15 g) black sesame seeds

Sift the flour in a large mixing bowl and add almond meal to combine. Set it aside. Place the butter, sugar and miso in a bowl and beat well until the color of the butter becomes whitish and creamy. I usually use a stand mixer with the whisk attachment. Break the egg into a small bowl and whisk a little bit until the egg white and egg yolk are mixed. Add a third of the egg to the mixing bowl and combine it with the butter and sugar. Add another third of the egg and beat well again. Add the last third of the egg and combine it with the mixture until it becomes silky and smooth. Change the mixer to a blade attachment and add the sifted flour and almond meal and sesame seeds to the bowl. Mix until it's just combined and you don't see any flour. Try not to overmix. Separate the dough in half and form them into two balls. Wrap the cookie dough in cling wrap and let it rest for 30 minutes in a refrigerator.

Preheat the oven to 350°F (180°C). Take the rested cookie dough out of the fridge. Roll the dough to ¼ inch (5 mm) thick and cut out with a cookie cutter. Place the cookies on a baking tray lined with parchment paper and bake for 20 to 25 minutes, or the until the cookie tops are browned slightly. Remove them from the oven and allow them to cool on a wire rack.

perfectly creamy no-churn miso ice cream

Add rich flavor to simple ice cream with some fermented miso. This is a super easy, no-churn ice cream recipe with a caramel-like flavor that is so creamy. I like to add some Japanese brown sugar syrup and soy bean powder, but you could also top it with some salted caramel sauce. Make this ahead of time as it takes 10 hours or more to allow the ice cream to freeze.

yield: 8 servings

2 cups (500 ml) heavy whipping cream

2 tbsp (30 g) white Basic Homemade Miso (page 10)

1⅓ cups (325 ml) sweetened condensed milk

To infuse the heavy whipping cream with the miso paste, pour the cream into a saucepan and heat over medium heat. When you start to see a few wisps of steam, turn the heat off. Scoop some of the cream into a ladle, then hold it over the saucepan and add the miso into the cream in the ladle. Dissolve the miso paste in the ladle by stirring with a pair of chopsticks or a spoon. Pour the mixture in the ladle back into the saucepan and stir. Strain out the miso solids using a strainer and refrigerate the cream until it is completely chilled again.

Pour the chilled heavy cream into the bowl of a stand mixer and whip the cream until it forms stiff peaks, for about 3 minutes, then set it aside. Pour the sweetened condensed milk into a separate mixing bowl. Scoop the heavy whipped cream and fold it into the condensed milk to lighten the condensed milk. Scrape the rest of the heavy whipped cream into the condensed milk and gently fold them together. It will look lumpy but keep folding gently until the mixture becomes smooth and only a few small lumps are seen.

Using a spatula, transfer the mixture into a freezer container. Cover the surface with parchment paper and put the container lid on. Freeze it for 10 hours or until it becomes solid. If you want a firmer ice cream, you can freeze it longer. If it becomes too firm, let it stand for 5 minutes before scooping. Eat within 2 weeks.

soft and moist miso pound cake

Adding miso to ordinary pound cake gives it a rich and elegant flavor. I like to eat this along with a simple, light tea to offset the richness. The almond meal gives this cake a soft, fluffy texture.

yield: 1 loaf

¾ cup (100 g) all-purpose flour

½ tsp baking powder

2½ tbsp (20 g) almond meal

½ cup (100 g) unsalted butter, room temperature

½ cup (100 g) sugar, divided

2 tbsp (30 g) white Basic Homemade Miso (page 10)

2 large eggs

¼ cup (30 g) crushed walnuts

1 tsp black sesame seeds

1 tsp white sesame seeds

Line a 4 x 9 x 2–inch (10 x 22 x 5–cm) cake tin with parchment paper and preheat the oven to 350°F (180°C).

Sift the flour and baking powder together in a bowl, then add the almond meal, mix and set it aside.

Place the softened butter into the bowl of a stand mixer and beat until it becomes creamy. Add the sugar 2 tablespoons (30 g) at a time and beat well after each addition; the butter should become white. Add the miso and mix well. Crack the eggs into a separate bowl and whisk them together. Add the whisked eggs a little bit at a time to the butter mixture and mix well each time. Add the dry ingredients and the walnuts into the batter and fold them in. Try not to overmix.

Pour the cake mixture into the prepared cake tin. Drop the tin lightly on the countertop a couple of times in order to release the air bubbles. Sprinkle the sesame seeds over the top of the cake. Place the pan in the oven and turn the heat down to 340°F (170°C). Bake for 50 minutes. After 10 minutes, remove the cake from the oven and score the center of the cake to create an even line for the cake to split a bit at the top when it bakes. Place it back in the oven to continue to bake for 40 minutes. Remove the cake from the tin and leave it to rest and cool on a rack before slicing.

note: This cake was made specifically in a 4 x 9 x 2–inch (10 x 22 x 5–cm) cake tin. You can also use an 8 x 4 x 6–inch (20 x 10 x 15–cm) loaf pan.

Rice Vinegar

for tasty home meals

Rice vinegar (komezu, or su) is made from fermented rice. It has a pale golden or yellow color and a mild flavor, which is why it goes well with the lightness and freshness of Japanese dishes. It is also less acidic than western vinegar, which is why western vinegars cannot be used as a substitute in these recipes. Soy sauce is a common Japanese condiment that many households around the world keep in their kitchen, but rice vinegar is another one that I believe is really essential for anyone who is interested in Japanese cooking. It can be used for sauces like ponzu, marinades for meat and to pickle vegetables (tsukemono).

Although rice vinegar can't really be made at home, nowadays it can be found in many grocery stores or you can find it at Asian markets. The most popular and well-known rice vinegar is by Mizkan, which still brews rice vinegar in its traditional way and is my favorite to use. You can use whichever brand you like, but just make sure that it is Japanese rice vinegar because it is different from others and it will affect the recipes and alter the flavor.

The most well-known Japanese food made with this fermented ingredient is sushi; simply add sugar and salt to rice vinegar and mix it with steamed rice and you have sushi rice! (See the recipe for Sushi Rice on page 169.) If you don't want to make your own sushi vinegar, you can buy rice vinegar pre-mixed with sugar and salt, which is called awasezu. You can also use rice vinegar as an alternative to other vinegars when making vinaigrettes because it's healthier and has a milder flavor, which will go perfectly on salads and with vegetables. However you choose to use it, rice vinegar is an essential for Japanese cooking.

simple homemade ponzu

Ponzu is a beloved sauce for many Japanese people because it adds a delicious tangy taste to a variety of dishes. You can easily buy bottled ponzu sauce in Japan because it's so popular, but it's also nice to make it yourself because you know exactly what's in it and it's easy. You can use this as a dressing, a dipping sauce and more!

yield: about 2 cups (500 ml)

1 cup (250 ml) soy sauce

1 cup (250 ml) rice vinegar

1 tbsp (15 ml) lemon zest

¼ cup (60 ml) mirin

1 tsp bonito flakes

1 tsp kelp strip

Place the soy sauce, rice vinegar, lemon zest, mirin, bonito flakes and kelp strip in a sterilized jar. Place the jar in the refrigerator and allow the bonito flakes and kelp to steep for 24 hours.

After 24 hours, drain the bonito flakes and kelp through a sieve and discard them. Pour the remaining sauce back into the jar and store it in the fridge. It will keep for about 6 months in the fridge.

healthy vinegared tomatoes

This is my favorite side dish because it's healthy and easy to add as a side with any meal. I sometimes also eat this for breakfast.

yield: 2 cups (about 300 g)

2 tbsp (30 ml) rice vinegar

1 tbsp (15 ml) olive oil

1 tbsp (15 ml) honey

2 cups (300 g) cherry tomatoes

1 tsp finely chopped ginger root

Combine the vinegar, olive oil and honey in a bowl. Whisk it all to combine, then set it aside. Score a tiny cross at the bottom of each tomato and blanch them in boiling water for 10 seconds, then refresh them in a bath of ice and water in a bowl. Drain that water. The tomatoes will start to self-peel from where you scored the cross at the bottom. Remove the remaining peel, then place the peeled tomatoes and finely chopped ginger root in a jar or container and pour the vinegar mixture over them. Marinate overnight.

inside-out sushi

(uramaki)

Sushi rolls are usually made with the seaweed wrapped around the outside. This is called makizushi. But when the rice is wrapped on the outside with the seaweed on the inside it is called uramaki, because it's inside-out. The flavor is essentially the same, but it's nice to prepare sushi this way because you can add toppings that can stick to the rice on the outer layer.

yield: 2 servings

2 sheets nori seaweed

3 cups (600 g) cooked Sushi Rice (page 169), divided

½ avocado, cut into sticks, divided

½ cucumber, cut into sticks, divided

4 sticks imitation crab meat (kanikama), divided

3 tsp (15 g) sesame seeds

2 tbsp (30 ml) soy sauce, to serve

Wasabi, to serve

Place a sheet of nori onto a sushi mat and place 1½ cups (300 g) of sushi rice on top. Wet your hands a bit, then spread the rice out with your hands to about ⅛ inch (3 mm) thick, leaving a ¾-inch (2-cm) gap along one long edge. Place cling wrap over the rice. Place a chopping board over the cling wrap and flip it all over. The sushi mat should now be on top.

Remove the mat and place half the avocado, cucumber and two crab meat sticks in a line on top of the seaweed sheet. Wet your fingertip with water or vinegar and run it along the ¾-inch (2-cm) gap of the seaweed sheet. Roll the sushi toward that edge by applying firm but gentle pressure, ensuring that the rice is firmly set as you roll.

Set the rolled sushi aside (I usually place it with the sealed side down so it can rest and stick more to hold the sushi together). Repeat for the remaining seaweed sheet. Sprinkle the sesame seeds over the top of both sushi rolls. Slice the rolls into rounds 1½ inches (4 cm) thick and serve with the soy sauce and a little bit of wasabi.

layered pork and cabbage hot pot with ponzu

This is the perfect winter dish to warm you up and share with family and friends. The layered cabbage resembles mille-feuille, so it's both visually pleasing and delicious. I think ponzu goes so well with cabbage and pork, and I often like to bring it all together in this hot pot.

yield: 4 servings

½ small head Napa cabbage, with stem attached

⅔ lb (300 g) pork belly, thinly sliced

2 cups (500 ml) Dashi with Bonito Flakes and Kelp (page 168)

2 tbsp (30 ml) sake

I tbsp (15 ml) soy sauce

I tsp grated ginger root

⅔ cup (140 ml) Simple Homemade Ponzu (page 72)

I cup (120 g) grated daikon radish

Seven-spice chili powder (shichimi togarashi), for garnish, optional

Cut the half head of cabbage in half and then in half again so that you have four lengthwise pieces. Layer the cabbage lengthwise, then lift two layers of cabbage and place two slices of pork on top. Repeat to place two slices of pork in between every two layers of cabbage. Repeat the same process for the rest of the pork and cabbage.

Cut the sandwiched pork and cabbage about 2 inches (5 cm) thick and cut the stem off. Pack the cut cabbage and pork vertically into the hot pot from the outer edge to the center. Pour the dashi stock, sake, soy sauce and ginger over the packed cabbage and pork. Place a lid on the pot and cook over medium heat. When it boils, turn the heat down to low and simmer for 30 minutes or until the cabbage softens.

This can be served on a table and eaten straight from the pot while it continues to cook. Serve the cabbage and pork with an individual small bowl of ponzu and grated daikon. Sprinkle it with chili powder if you like.

note: Shichimi togarashi is a spice mixture containing seven types of spices ("shichi" means "seven" in Japanese). It usually contains red chili pepper, Japanese pepper, orange peel, black and white sesame seeds, ginger and seaweed. It differs from ichimi togarashi, which is simply ground red chili. Shichimi togarashi is commonly used as a seasoning to add a spicy kick to dishes.

mushroom sauté dressed with ponzu

This is a super yummy and healthy dish to eat as a side or with a variety of other small dishes like we do in Japan. It's very easy and doesn't take long at all to pull together.

yield: 4 servings

3½ oz (100 g) enoki mushrooms

3½ oz (100 g) shimeji mushrooms

1 tbsp (15 g) butter

1 cup (120 g) grated daikon, divided

2 tbsp (30 g) finely chopped scallions, for garnish

Shredded seaweed, for garnish

4 tbsp (60 ml) Simple Homemade Ponzu (page 72), divided, for garnish

Separate the enoki and shimeji mushrooms with your hands and cut the enoki in half lengthwise. Heat the butter in a frying pan and sauté the mushrooms for 3 minutes.

Turn the heat off and divide the mushrooms into four separate small bowls. Top each bowl with ¼ cup (30 g) of grated daikon. Scatter the scallions and shredded seaweed on top and dress each bowl with 1 tablespoon (15 ml) of ponzu.

note: Enoki mushrooms are a type of Japanese mushroom that are small and white with a small cap.

ground chicken meatball stew with ponzu sauce

This is one of my favorite winter comfort foods. Adding chicken meatballs to hot pots is very common in Japan. I personally like it because the meat is leaner than regular meatballs, and the chicken meatballs go better with ponzu. We like to eat this stew right from the hot pot and dip the meatballs straight into the ponzu sauce for a warm but refreshing, tangy bite.

yield: 2 servings

⅔ lb (300 g) ground chicken

1 egg

½ tsp salt

1 tbsp (15 g) potato starch (katakuriko)

6 shiitake mushrooms

5¼ cups (1.25 L) water

1 (2-inch [5-cm]) piece kombu kelp

2 tbsp (30 ml) sake

6 oz (170 g) tofu (about ½ block)

¼ Napa cabbage, cut into 2-inch (5-cm) pieces

1 leek, sliced diagonally into large pieces

Salt, to taste

1 cup (250 ml) Simple Homemade Ponzu (page 72)

2 cups (240 g) grated daikon

Seven-spice chili powder (shichimi togarashi), optional

To make the chicken meatballs, mix the ground chicken in a large mixing bowl with the egg, salt and potato starch. Knead with your hands, then roll the mixture into small golf ball–sized meatballs. Set them aside.

Remove the stems from the shiitake mushrooms and score a cross on the surface of each mushroom. Set them aside.

Pour the water, kombu kelp and sake in a hot pot and heat over medium heat. When it boils, skim the foam off the surface and remove the kombu kelp. Add the chicken meatballs gently into the pot. Remove the foam as necessary with a sieve. Add the tofu, Napa cabbage, leek, salt and shiitake mushrooms into the pot. When it boils, turn the heat to low and place a lid over it. Simmer for 15 minutes.

Pour ½ cup (120 ml) of ponzu sauce into each of two small serving bowls. Add the grated daikon and sprinkle some chili powder if you prefer a little bit of a spicy kick. We usually cook this hot pot on a portable stove set on the table and eat it straight from the pot while it is still cooking. Dip the cooked meatballs and veggies in the ponzu sauce to eat.

healthy and fresh octopus and cucumber salad

(sunomono)

This is a light pickled dish that you can eat on the side or on its own. The savory dressing has a peppery sweetness that complements this salad perfectly.

yield: 2 servings

1 English or Lebanese cucumber, thinly sliced

1 tsp salt

2 tsp (10 ml) rice vinegar

2 tsp (10 ml) soy sauce

2 tsp (10 ml) mirin

2 tsp (10 ml) water

1 tsp ginger juice

¼ lb (100 g) cooked octopus, cut into small pieces

1 tsp ginger root, cut into thin sticks, for garnish

Sesame seeds, for garnish

Place the sliced cucumber in a mixing bowl and toss it with the salt to coat the slices evenly. Let it rest for 10 minutes, then squeeze the water out of the cucumbers with your hands. Discard the water.

In a separate mixing bowl, combine the vinegar, soy sauce, mirin, water and ginger juice. Add the octopus pieces and the cucumber. Toss it all together and then serve in small bowls. Garnish with the ginger sticks and sesame seeds.

soft tofu and chicken burgers with ponzu sauce

I love to add tofu when I make hamburgers because it makes them so much softer and juicier and doesn't compromise the flavor. This is one of my go-to recipes because it's so simple, it tastes good every time and it's healthy. Elizabeth and I always pack the leftovers for lunch the next day.

yield: 2 servings

2 cups (500 ml) water

12 oz (340 g) firm tofu

⅓ lb (150 g) ground chicken

4 shiso leaves, finely chopped

1 tbsp (15 g) potato starch (katakuriko)

¼ tsp salt

¼ tsp pepper

1 tbsp (15 ml) olive oil

Green salad leaves, to serve

½ cup (60 g) grated daikon radish

4 tbsp (60 ml) Simple Homemade Ponzu (page 72), divided

Bring the water in a saucepan or a pot to a boil over high heat, then add the tofu. Turn the heat down to medium and cook the tofu for 5 minutes. Drain the tofu and place it on a heatproof dish lined with a paper towel. Cover the tofu with another piece of paper towel and place a weight on top (such as a plate). Leave it for 10 minutes, until the moisture is removed from the tofu. Break it apart with your hands into a mixing bowl. Add the chicken, shiso leaves, potato starch, salt and pepper to the tofu and combine it all together by kneading with your hands. Roll the mixture into four equal, flat oval-shaped patties.

Heat the olive oil in a saucepan over medium heat, add the patties and cook one side for 5 minutes, then flip them over and cook the other side for 5 minutes. Press on a patty and if clear juice comes out, it is done. Serve on top of green salad leaves on a plate. Top with grated daikon and pour 1 tablespoon (15 ml) of ponzu over each patty.

pickled daikon radish with zesty yuzu

Pickled daikon tastes amazing on its own, but adding yuzu gives it a tasty and zesty citrus tang that makes it even better. Yuzu is a really unique citrus and if you can find it, that would be best for this recipe. If you can't find it, you can substitute with another citrus like lemon, but the flavor will be a bit different.

yield: 1 lb (454 g)

1 lb (454 g) daikon radish, sliced thinly

2 tbsp plus ½ tsp (34 g) salt, divided

3 tbsp (45 ml) rice vinegar

2 tbsp (30 ml) mirin

1 tbsp (15 g) sugar

1 tbsp (15 g) yuzu peel

½ tbsp (3 g) shredded kombu kelp

Place the daikon radish in a mixing bowl, sprinkle with 2 tablespoons (30 g) of salt and toss to coat evenly. Set it aside for 10 minutes, then squeeze water out of the daikon radish with your hands. Discard the water.

Place the rice vinegar, mirin, sugar and ½ teaspoon of salt in a saucepan. Heat the vinegar mix over high heat and when it boils, turn the heat off and remove it from the heat. Set it aside to let it cool down.

Put the radish, yuzu peel, kombu kelp and vinegar mix in a ziplock bag and seal the bag. Massage the radish and vinegar mix in the bag with your hands, leave it for 15 minutes and then serve. It will keep for a week refrigerated.

vibrant rainbow roll sushi

This sushi is very popular at sushi restaurants around the world because it's not only colorful and pretty to look at; it's also so delicious. Using the freshest sushi-grade fish you can get will make this sushi much better and tastier. Of course, it's always important when consuming raw fish that you make sure that it is sushi or sashimi-grade when you purchase it.

yield: 2 rolls

2 nori seaweed sheets, divided

3 cups (600 g) cooked Sushi Rice (page 169), divided

¼ English or Lebanese cucumber, cut into sticks, divided

4 crab cake sticks (kanikama), divided

½ avocado, thinly sliced

2 oz (50 g) sashimi-grade yellowfin tuna, thinly sliced

2 oz (50 g) cooked prawns

1 fried egg, cut into strips

2 oz (50 g) sashimi-grade salmon, thinly sliced

2 tsp (10 g) sesame seeds, divided

2 tbsp (30 ml) soy sauce, to serve

Wasabi, to serve

Place a sheet of seaweed onto a sushi mat and place half of the cooked sushi rice on top. Wet your hands a bit with water and spread the rice out with your wet hands to about ⅕ inch (5 mm) thick, leaving ½ inch (1 cm) on one long edge. Place cling wrap over the rice. Place another sushi mat or a chopping board on top of the cling wrap and flip it all over. Remove the top sushi mat off the seaweed sheet. Place half the amount of cucumber sticks and 2 crab sticks in a line along the center of the seaweed sheet. Wet your fingertip with water and run your finger along the ½-inch (1-cm) edge of seaweed that you left without rice. Roll the sushi toward that edge, applying firm but gentle pressure as you roll. Once you've rolled it to the edge, press gently but tightly to seal it together. Set it aside.

Line the bamboo sushi rolling mat with a piece of cling wrap. Lay it flat on the counter or on a chopping board. Arrange half of the avocado, tuna, prawns, egg strips and salmon on the cling wrap. Allow each piece to overlap a little bit. Place the rolled sushi onto the arranged ingredients and use the cling wrap to wrap and roll them together. Sprinkle half of the sesame seeds on top. Repeat for the remaining amount of rice and fillings. Slice the roll into rounds of about 1 inch (3 cm) and serve with a small bowl of soy sauce and a little bit of wasabi.

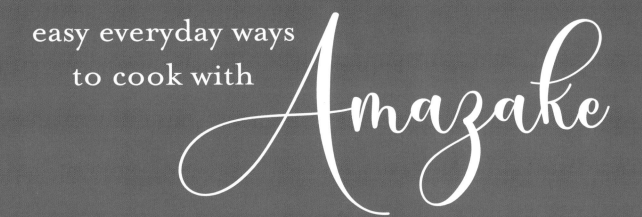

easy everyday ways to cook with *Amazake*

Amazake is by far one of my favorite Japanese drinks. Elizabeth and I love to drink this every morning whenever we can, or eat it in Healthy and Simple Oatmeal Amazake (page 97) to give us energy for the day.

Amazake, a sweet, fermented drink, is very popular in Japan because of its nutritional benefits, and is considered by many as a "beauty drink" because of the many beneficial vitamins and nutrients that it contains. Along with vitamins B_1, B_2 and B_6, amazake also contains folic acid, dietary fiber, arginine, glutamine, glucose, oligosaccharide and cysteine. These are all essential components in maintaining the wellness of your body and promoting healthy immune and digestive systems. Amazake is also beneficial to the skin, as the vitamin B's that it contains activate the turnover of skin cells— which is why Japanese women love to drink it to maintain a healthy and youthful complexion.

Amazake is part of the group of fermented Japanese foods made from the *Aspergillus oryzae* fungus mold, commonly known as koji. You can make amazake using kome koji, which is a rice koji and is the type of amazake you'll make in this book, or sake kasu, which is derived from the lees (residue) left over from the production of sake. As sake kasu amazake comes from sake lees, it does contain a low amount of alcohol and requires additional sugar to make it sweet. However, kome koji amazake contains no alcohol and is naturally sweetened when the rice is fermented with koji, which I prefer. I used to drink a cup of sake kasu amazake to keep me warm during the cold winter and it was always very comforting.

Because of its popularity in Japan, amazake is readily available to buy; however, it is also easy to make at home. You can drink amazake just as it is, either hot or cold, or you can use it in a variety of savory dishes, desserts and more.

homemade amazake

Amazake is my favorite traditional sweet drink. It reminds me of my time working as a nurse in Japan and still always comforts me and makes me feel very warm and cozy. To make this, you will just need kome koji, which you can buy online or in supermarkets, and some sort of incubator to keep the amazake at around 150° to 160°F (65° to 70°C). My favorite methods are to use either a rice cooker or a yogurt maker. You could also use a thermal pot or an oven.

yield: 1 cup (250 ml)
fermentation time: 6 to 8 hours

½ cup (100 g) koji

¾ cup (180 ml) hot water

Place the koji in a bowl. Pour 150° to 160°F (65° to 70°C) hot water into the bowl and mix well. Check the mixture temperature to make sure it is around 150°F (65°C). Place the mixture into a rice cooker, yogurt maker, oven, etc.—anything that can keep it at 150°F (65°C)—and leave it for about 6 to 8 hours, stirring occasionally. I stir the mixture at 4 hours in, to make sure it is all fermented evenly.

Stop whatever machine you used and put the amazake into a pan over medium heat for 5 minutes after it has cooked for 8 hours (do not let the temperature go above 175°F (80°C). By doing this, it will stop any further fermentation. Pour it into a sterilized jar and keep it refrigerated for up to 10 days. Serve hot or leave it in the fridge to cool and serve cold.

note: You can also keep amazake in the freezer for up to 3 months.

healthy and simple oatmeal amazake

Amazake or oats on their own are great for breakfast, but I like to combine the two to make an even healthier and more energizing meal to get me ready for the day. The amazake brings a natural sweetness to the oats and makes the texture smoother. You can top it with seasonal fruits and berries, if you like.

yield: 2 bowls

⅔ cup (50 g) oatmeal

1¼ cups (300 ml) water

½ cup (100 g) koji

Place the oatmeal and water into a saucepan and bring it to a boil. Turn the heat off and occasionally stir it while it cools down. Check the temperature and when it cools to 160°F (70°C), add the koji. Place the mixture in an oven, rice cooker, yogurt maker, etc.—anything that will keep the mixture at 140°F (60°C) for 7 hours so that the koji can ferment.

After 7 hours, place the mixture into a saucepan and bring it to a boil so that the fermentation will stop. Once it comes to a boil, remove the pot from the heat and keep the oatmeal amazake in an airtight container for up to 10 days.

basic brown rice amazake

I sometimes like to add brown rice to my amazake to thicken it and make it into a sweet but healthy rice porridge.

yield: 2 bowls

¾ cup (150 g) cooked brown rice

1¼ cups (300 ml) water

½ cup (100 g) koji

Place the cooked rice in a bowl. Pour the water, heated to 150° to 160°F (65° to 70°C), into the bowl and mix with the cooked rice. Add the koji to the bowl and combine well. Check the mixture's temperature to make sure it is around 140°F (60°C). Place the mixture into a rice cooker, yogurt maker, oven, etc.—anything that can keep it at 140°F (60°C)—and leave it for about 6 to 8 hours, stirring occasionally (I stir at the 4-hour mark). If you're using a rice cooker, set it to keep warm and leave the lid slightly open with a kitchen cloth covering the top.

After 6 to 8 hours, stop whatever machine you used to keep the rice amazake warm, then put it into a pan over medium heat for 5 minutes; do not let the temperature go above 175°F (80°C). Doing this will stop any further fermentation. Pour the rice amazake into a sterilized jar and keep it refrigerated for up to 10 days, or in a freezer for 3 months. Serve hot or leave in the fridge to cool and serve cold.

baked salmon with amazake marinade

Marinating salmon with miso is my favorite way to eat it, and adding amazake makes it even better. The koji from the amazake makes the salmon softer and more tender and adds delicious flavor. It goes perfectly with steamed white rice and some salad.

yield: 2 servings

¼ cup (60 g) Homemade Amazake (page 94)

1 tbsp (15 g) white Basic Homemade Miso (page 10)

2 salmon fillets, ¼ –⅓ lb (100–150 g) each

Preheat the oven to 350°F (180°C). Mix the amazake and miso together in a small bowl. Place the salmon fillets into a ziplock bag and pour the amazake-miso mixture into the bag. Close the bag and rub it to soak the mixture into the salmon. Leave it to marinate overnight or for a minimum of 4 hours.

After it's marinated, remove the salmon from the marinade and place it onto a baking tray lined with parchment paper. Bake for 30 minutes. Turn off the oven, remove the salmon and serve.

amazake teriyaki chicken

Cooking teriyaki chicken with amazake is another way that I like to spice up plain teriyaki chicken. The koji from the amazake tenderizes the chicken and the chicken skin adds a crispiness that makes it such a delicious dish. This is a weeknight winner for me when I don't have much energy or time to cook because it only has three ingredients and is really simple to make.

yield: 2 servings

2 chicken thighs, skin on

½ cup (120 g) Homemade Amazake (page 94)

¼ cup (60 ml) soy sauce

Pierce the chicken thighs with a fork and score/slice the thighs. Open it up to make the meat even on both sides and to allow the sauce to distribute easily. Combine the amazake and soy sauce in a bowl and marinate the chicken thighs for 1 hour.

Heat a frying pan over low heat. Place the chicken in the pan skin side down (no oil necessary), and grill it for about 5 minutes. Flip the chicken over and grill for another 5 minutes on the other side. Once both sides are browned and the skin is crispy, remove the chicken from the heat and slice it into strips.

amazake tamagoyaki

Tamagoyaki is a simple but versatile Japanese egg dish that can be used in bento, sushi, sandwiches and more. A small rectangular pan works best to achieve a rectangular shape of the egg, or you can try to use a round one and fold in the sides of the egg to make a rectangle. Usually this is made with sugar, but the amazake takes its place here and makes it healthier and naturally sweet.

yield: 2 servings

3 eggs

1½ tbsp (22 g) Homemade Amazake (page 94)

½ tsp salt

2 tbsp (30 ml) water

2 tbsp (30 ml) plus 2 tsp (10 ml) olive oil, divided

Crack the eggs into a small- to medium-size mixing bowl and whisk them. Add the amazake, salt and water and whisk together gently to avoid too many bubbles forming. Pour about 2 tablespoons (30 ml) of olive oil into a small mixing bowl and soak a paper towel in the oil, then set it aside.

Heat 2 teaspoons (10 ml) of olive oil in a round or rectangular frying pan over medium heat until you can feel the heat when you hover your hand over the pan. Pour a third of the egg mixture into the pan (you should hear a sizzling sound). Break any bubbles that have formed with the edge of a fork or chopsticks, and scramble gently and slightly. When the egg has solidified a little, fold and push the egg to one end of the pan.

Wipe the empty side of the pan with the oil-soaked paper towel and pour another third of the egg mixture into the empty space of the pan. Lift the folded egg up to let the egg mixture run under it. Fold and roll the egg from one side of the pan and wipe the empty space of the pan with the oil-soaked paper towel. Pour the last third of the egg mixture and repeat the fold and roll. Turn the heat off and wrap the rolled egg with paper towels. Roll the wrapped egg roll with a sushi mat to shape it and rest to cool down. Once it is cool, slice it into pieces about 1 inch (3 cm) thick and serve.

mango amazake summer smoothie

This is such an easy thing to make when you have ready-made amazake on hand. The mango brings a tropical sweetness to the amazake that makes it so refreshing and tasty.

yield: 1 serving

¾ cup (180 g) Homemade Amazake (page 94)

½ mango, peeled and sliced, plus more to serve

Mint leaf, for garnish

Sprinkle of oats, for garnish

Chia seeds, for garnish

Add the amazake and mango slices into a blender and mix until smooth. Serve in a glass with extra mango chunks. Garnish with the mint leaf, oats and chia seeds.

soft amazake kinako mochi

This dessert is simple and healthier than most because the amazake has a natural sweetness so it is not necessary to add any sugar. The mochi has so much flavor, and the soy bean powder (kinako) matches so well and tastes even better if you add some brown sugar syrup (kuromitsu) over the top, which you can make or buy online or in Japanese grocery stores.

yield: 2 servings

½ cup (120 g) Homemade Amazake (page 94)

2 tbsp (30 g) potato starch (katakuriko)

1 tbsp (15 g) soy bean powder (kinako)

Brown sugar syrup (kuromitsu), optional

Put the amazake in a blender with a little bit of water and blend until it is smooth. Pour it into a saucepan and heat over low heat. Add the potato starch and continuously stir until it becomes thickened and sticks together, 2 to 3 minutes.

Remove the pan from the heat and pour it into a container. Allow it to cool down a bit, then put it in the fridge to set for an hour. Once it is set, cube it and put it into a bowl, and sprinkle the soy bean powder on top. Add brown sugar syrup on top, if desired.

sweet amazake custard pudding

This is a really tasty pudding that is naturally sweetened by the amazake so it doesn't require much sugar. You can drizzle it with brown sugar syrup (kuromitsu) or caramel and serve it with warm tea for a sweet little treat.

yield: 3 servings

2 large eggs

¾ cup (180 ml) milk

3 tbsp (45 g) Homemade Amazake (page 94)

1 tbsp (15 g) sugar

Brown sugar syrup (kuromitsu) or caramel, to serve

Crack the eggs into a mixing bowl and add the milk. Whisk it together to make it smooth, then strain it through a sieve into another bowl. Add the amazake and sugar and mix together. Divide it into three ramekins and set it aside.

Boil some water in a large pot and place a steamer on top of the boiling water. Place the ramekins into the steamer and steam for 15 minutes. Turn the heat off and remove the ramekins.

Let them cool down a bit, then put them in the fridge for at least an hour. Once they're cold, drizzle each with brown sugar syrup or caramel to serve.

amazake matcha sweet rice balls

(ohagi)

These sweet rice balls (ohagi) are traditional little Japanese confectionary sweets (wagashi). They are usually made with glutinous rice and sweet red bean paste, so these are a little twist using amazake and matcha.

yield: 10 balls

¾ cup (150 g) uncooked short-grain Japanese koshihikari rice

½ cup (120 g) Homemade Amazake (page 94)

½ cup (120 ml) water

2 tbsp (30 g) matcha

1 tbsp (15 g) confectioners' sugar

Wash the rice and drain it. Cook the rice with the amazake and water in a rice cooker or pot. Once the rice is cooked, put it into a bowl and mash it a bit to combine the grains.

Divide the rice into 10 equal-sized balls, about 3 tablespoons (45 g) each. Wrap the rice balls with cling wrap and shape them into round circles. Combine the matcha and confectioners' sugar, remove the cling wrap from the rice balls and sprinkle the matcha and sugar mixture over the tops.

sweet steamed buns (mushi pan) with amazake

Mushi pan are soft and light little Japanese steamed sponge cakes. I like to make these because they are very easy to prepare and very versatile, so you can adapt them in many ways. For these, I added some amazake for natural sweetness.

yield: 6 buns

1 cup (125 g) all-purpose flour

1 tsp baking powder

1 cup (240 g) Homemade Amazake (page 94)

Sprinkle of black sesame seeds

Line a muffin tray with six muffin baking cups. Sift the flour and baking powder together into a mixing bowl. Make a well in the center and fold the amazake into the flour. Be careful not to overmix.

Divide the mixture into the six muffin baking cups. Sprinkle black sesame seeds on the top of each mushi pan. Steam for 15 minutes in a steamer over boiling water. Poke a skewer through one of the cakes to test if they are ready. If it comes out clean, you can remove them from the heat and serve.

note: If you like a smooth texture, you can blitz the amazake in a food processor beforehand.

amazake bubble tea

Bubble tea is a great refreshing drink but it can be full of sugars and syrups. These are much healthier versions that have the natural sweetness from amazake. You can choose the milk version or the matcha version; both use amazake to add some delicious natural flavor.

yield: 4 servings

milk bubble tea

⅓ cup (50 g) black tapioca pearls

1¼ cups (300 ml) water plus more, divided

1 tbsp (15 g) brown sugar

2 cups (480 g) Homemade Amazake (page 94)

1⅔ cups (400 ml) soy, almond or other preferred milk

matcha bubble tea

⅓ cup (50 g) white tapioca pearls

1¼ cups (300 ml) water plus more, divided

1 tbsp (15 g) super-fine sugar, or caster sugar

1 tbsp (15 g) matcha powder

1⅔ cups and ½ tbsp (407 ml) hot water, divided

2 cups (480 g) Homemade Amazake (page 94)

For the milk bubble tea, place the tapioca pearls and water in a pot over medium heat. When the water boils, turn the heat down to low and simmer for 1½ hours. Turn the heat off and drain the cooking water. Place the drained tapioca back into the pot and add enough water to cover it. Add the brown sugar and bring the tapioca mixture to a boil over medium heat. Turn the heat down and cook for 5 minutes. Turn the heat off and transfer it all to a bowl, including the sugar water. The sugary water will help to prevent the tapioca from sticking together as it dries. Cool it completely in the fridge for 30 minutes.

Place the amazake and the milk in a blender. Pulse a few times to combine them. Scoop and divide the tapioca into four glasses and pour the blended amazake milk into the glasses.

For the matcha bubble tea, place the tapioca and the water in a pot over medium heat. When the water boils, turn the heat down to low and simmer for 1½ hours. Turn the heat off and drain the cooking water. Place the drained tapioca back into the pot and add enough water to cover it. Add the sugar and bring the tapioca mixture to a boil over medium heat. Turn the heat down and cook for 5 minutes. Turn the heat off and transfer it all to a bowl, including the sugar water. The sugary water will help to prevent the tapioca from sticking together as it dries. Cool it completely in the fridge for 30 minutes.

Place the matcha powder in a bowl and add ½ tablespoon (7 ml) of hot water to make a paste. Stir it to mix well. Gradually add 1⅔ cups (400 ml) hot water, stirring so lumps don't form and the mixture stays smooth. Place the amazake and the matcha mixture in a blender and pulse a few times to blend it together. Scoop and divide the tapioca into four glasses and pour the amazake-matcha mixture over the top.

amazake pancakes

Traditional pancakes are so good because they are perfect for breakfast or dessert. They're already delicious and made even better here because they're naturally sweetened with amazake instead of sugar.

yield: 2 servings

¾ cup (100 g) all-purpose flour

1 tsp baking powder

½ cup (120 g) Homemade Amazake (page 94)

1 egg

Pinch of salt

2 tsp (10 g) butter, to serve

Maple syrup, to serve, optional

Any toppings you like such as strawberries, bananas, etc., optional

Sift the flour and baking powder together and set it aside. Place the amazake in a blender and blend for 30 seconds on low speed to make the amazake smooth.

Whisk the egg in a mixing bowl, then add the amazake and a pinch of salt and combine them. Add the sifted flour and baking powder to the bowl and combine them all together. Try not to overmix. The batter will be thick, making thick pancakes.

Spray cooking oil in a frying pan, then heat the frying pan over medium heat. Pour a sixth of the pancake batter into the frying pan. Cook 1 or 2 at a time. When the batter starts to bubble, turn the pancake over with a spatula and cook the other side for 3 minutes. Cook the rest of the pancakes, for a total of six. Stack three pancakes on each plate and top with the butter and the maple syrup and chosen toppings, if using.

naturally sweet amazake lemonade

This is such a refreshing and sweet drink with a zesty flavor from the lemon. I love to drink amazake this way during warmer days.

yield: 2 servings

1¾ cups (420 g) Homemade Amazake (page 94)

2 tbsp (30 ml) lemon juice

2 tsp (10 ml) honey, optional

2 wedges of lemon, for garnish

Divide the amazake equally into two glasses. Add equal parts of lemon juice and honey (if using) to each glass and stir. Top the glasses with a wedge of lemon.

cool and refreshing amazake kiwi granita

Granitas are super refreshing and delicious drinks because they are semi-frozen and sweet. This Amazake Kiwi Granita is even better because it's naturally sweet and healthier with amazake, while still being so tasty. It's the perfect drink to cool you down on hot summer days.

yield: 2 servings

2 kiwi fruits, plus extra slices for garnish

⅔ cup (160 g) Homemade Amazake (page 94)

Mint leaves, for garnish

Peel the 2 kiwis and cut them into small pieces. Place the amazake and the cut kiwi fruit into a blender and blend until smooth. Pour the mixture into a shallow freeze-proof container and freeze it for 1 hour.

Take the container out of the freezer and break up the ice crystals with a fork, then return it to the freezer. Repeat breaking it up every 30 minutes until it achieves a gravel-like texture. Serve in two glasses and garnish it with kiwi slices and mint leaves.

simple and scrumptious dishes using

Shio Koji

Shio koji is a natural and fermented Japanese seasoning made from just three ingredients: rice koji, salt and water. Shio koji has been used for many years in Japan and has recently become very trendy due to the increased popularity of fermented foods and their health benefits. I have definitely been one of the people to jump on the shio koji bandwagon because of how amazing and healthy it is.

Shio koji, like other fermented foods, is high in vitamins and minerals and is naturally probiotic. It is also lower in sodium compared to soy sauce and table salt, which is why it is great to use in their place to maintain a subtle salty flavor while reducing your salt intake.

Shio koji is also very rich in enzymes that break down both proteins and starches, which brings out the umami richness in foods and tenderizes meat and fish. It's no surprise shio koji is so popular. I've discovered it is quite simple to make at home, and I like to use as much as I can when I cook. Once I see that my shio koji stock

is running low, I prepare a new batch to make sure I have some available while waiting for the new batch to ferment. If you can't or don't want to make it at home, you can definitely use a store-bought shio koji to make any of the following recipes. But I definitely think it's worthwhile to make it yourself because it's easy and fun to prepare.

This traditional condiment can be used as a multipurpose seasoning for a range of dishes, but it is primarily used as a marinade for meats and fish, like Crispy Shio Koji Karaage (page 129) and Fresh Shio Koji–Marinated Seafood Poke Bowls (page 141). However you choose to use the shio koji, you'll appreciate the healthy versatility it offers as a staple seasoning.

homemade shio koji

This is a recipe for basic shio koji that is easy and fun to prepare. Once you have made this you can store it in the fridge and use it to season meats and fish. I recommend you make your shio koji in the warmer months because you need to keep it in a room above 68°F (20°C) during its fermentation.

yield: 1 cup (250 ml)
fermentation time: 1 week

½ cup (100 g) rice koji

2 tbsp (30 g) salt

Place the rice koji in a mixing bowl and add the salt, then combine well with your hands. Put the rice koji and salt in a glass jar and add enough water just to cover. Place a lid on top and leave it in a warm room with a temperature above 68°F (20°C) for a week. Stir the mixture once a day with a wooden spoon. It will be ready to use when the rice koji is softened and has a sweet mellow fragrance. Store it in the fridge to avoid further fermentation, and it will keep refrigerated for about 6 months.

crispy shio koji karaage

Karaage is the best Japanese fried chicken. The flavors in the marinade make the chicken so tasty, and unlike the typical fried chicken breading of breadcrumbs, flour and egg, this uses just potato starch, so it's much easier. Although thigh meat is often used for frying chicken because it has more flavor and is juicier, I use chicken breast in this recipe because the koji tenderizes the meat and maintains the flavor and tenderness.

yield: 2 servings

⅔ cup (300 g) chicken breast, chopped small

2 tbsp (30 g) Homemade Shio Koji (page 126)

1 tsp grated ginger root

1 tsp minced garlic

1 tsp soy sauce

Sesame or vegetable oil, for frying

½ cup (80 g) potato starch (katakuriko)

Place the chicken, shio koji, ginger, garlic and soy sauce in a ziplock bag and zip it shut. Gently squish the ingredients together to marinate the meat. Leave it to marinate for 20 minutes.

Once it has marinated, heat up enough oil in a frying pan to deep-fry the chicken. Heat the oil to 320°F (160°C). While the oil is heating, remove the chicken from the marinade and coat it with potato starch. Dust off the excess potato starch and deep-fry the chicken in batches (don't put all the chicken into the oil at once). Since the chicken is chopped into small pieces, it shouldn't take long to cook. Once it is browned and looking crispy, 3 to 5 minutes, it should be done.

creamy mushroom soup with shio koji

Cozy up with this creamy mushroom and bacon soup. The added touch of subtle saltiness and flavor from the shio koji makes it so tasty. The soup goes perfectly with some toasted bread rolls.

yield: 2 servings

½ cup (50 g) broccoli

½ tbsp (7 g) butter

2½ tbsp (25 g) finely chopped onion

1 tsp minced garlic

1 tsp grated ginger root

2 slices uncooked bacon, chopped small

1 cup (100 g) shimeji mushrooms

1 tbsp (10 g) all-purpose flour

1½ cups (360 ml) water

1½ cups (360 ml) milk

1 tbsp (15 g) Homemade Shio Koji (page 126)

Parboil the broccoli and set it aside. Heat the butter, onion, garlic and ginger in a large saucepan. Once it becomes fragrant, add the bacon to the pan. When the bacon is cooked and browned, add the shimeji mushrooms. Once the mushrooms are softened, 2 to 3 minutes, add the flour and stir, then add the water, milk and shio koji and stir. Bring the soup to a boil, then turn the heat down. Add the broccoli and simmer for 2 minutes. Remove it from the heat and serve.

juicy shio koji japanese hamburgers

A simple dish that's sure to please, these hamburgers have the added benefit of shio koji to keep them juicy. You can serve them with many different types of sauces and a side of salad and rice for an easy and healthy dinner.

yield: 2 servings

2 tbsp (30 ml) olive oil, divided

⅔ cup (100 g) finely chopped onion

⅔ cup (300 g) ground beef

2 tbsp (30 g) Homemade Shio Koji (page 126)

1 egg

2½ tbsp (20 g) panko breadcrumbs

Heat 1 tablespoon (15 ml) of olive oil and cook the onion until it is translucent, softened and a bit caramelized, 3 to 5 minutes. Remove the onion from the heat and allow it to cool down.

Place the ground beef, shio koji, egg, panko crumbs and the cooled onion in a mixing bowl and squish together with your hands to combine them well. Divide the mixture into four sections and mold each into flat oval shapes.

Heat 1 tablespoon (15 ml) of olive oil in a frying pan over medium heat and cook the hamburgers for 3 minutes on each side, or until both sides are browned. When you press on the hamburger and the juice comes out clear, then it is cooked and ready.

shio koji—marinated fish fry

I make my own version of classic fish and chips by pairing this shio koji—marinated fried fish with lotus root (renkon) chips. You can make your own fried lotus root chips or buy a frozen package from an Asian market, which is a lot easier. Marinating the fish in shio koji makes it juicy inside and crunchy outside.

yield: 2 servings

2 white fish fillets, such as swordfish or hoki

1 tbsp (15 g) Homemade Shio Koji (page 126)

1 large egg

¼ cup (60 ml) water

1 tbsp (15 g) Japanese mayonnaise

4 tbsp (35 g) all-purpose flour

1 cup (120 g) panko breadcrumbs

2 cups (500 ml) sesame or vegetable oil, for deep-frying

Green salad leaves, to serve

Potato or lotus root (renkon) chips, to serve, optional

Place the fish fillets in a ziplock bag and add the shio koji. Zip the bag and massage the koji well into the fish fillets. Refrigerate the fish fillets for 1 hour to let them marinate.

About 10 minutes before taking the marinated fish fillets out of the fridge, make the deep-frying batter. Crack the egg into a mixing bowl and add the water and mayonnaise. Combine it well, then add the flour and mix it all together. Pour the panko crumbs into a shallow tray or dish. Dip the fish fillets into the batter to coat them, then transfer them to the panko tray to cover them on both sides with panko crumbs.

Heat the oil in a deep-frying pan over medium heat. Drop a small piece of panko crumb into the oil to check its temperature. If it sinks halfway and floats back up with small bubbles around it, it is ready to deep-fry. Deep-fry the panko-crumbed fish fillets; when they are lightly browned, about 3 to 5 minutes depending on how thick the fish fillets are, they are cooked. Serve with a green salad and potato chips or renkon chips.

rice balls with shio koji and pickled plum

Pickled plum (umeboshi) is a really classic and slightly sour but delicious filling for rice balls (onigiri) in Japan. You'll find these at any store, but to make it less basic I like to add shio koji. Adding shio koji helps the rice to retain moisture so it will not get dry even when it is cooled down. It also gives the rice a tasty, mellow saltiness.

yield: 6 rice balls

2 cups (400 g) uncooked Japanese short-grain koshihikari rice

1½ cups (360 ml) water

1 tbsp (15 g) Homemade Shio Koji (page 126)

3 pickled plums, for garnish

6 strips of nori seaweed

Wash the rice and drain the water. Place the washed rice in a rice cooker and add the water and the shio koji. Give it a stir with a wooden spoon and turn on the rice cooker.

While the rice is being cooked, prepare the plums. Deseed the pickled plums and mash them together, then divide that into six portions. When the rice is cooked, prepare a rice bowl lined with cling wrap. Put a sixth of the cooked rice in the wrap and squeeze and shape it into a triangle or circle. It will be hot but it's better to be shaped at this time. Repeat with the rest of the rice to make six rice balls. Top them with pickled plum and wrap them with seaweed.

note: If you do not have a rice cooker, the Japanese short-grain koshihikari rice can be cooked in a large pot. Use equal parts of rice and water and simmer it over low-medium heat for about 30 minutes without opening the lid. After the 30 minutes, turn off the heat and let the rice rest for 10 minutes before opening the lid.

super simple shio koji–pickled cucumbers

This delicious and healthy cucumber is easy to pickle with shio koji.

yield: 2 cups (300 g)

1 English or Lebanese cucumber

1 tbsp (15 g) Homemade Shio Koji (page 126)

Wash and trim both ends of the cucumber. Cut the cucumber in half. Place both halves in a ziplock bag and add the shio koji. Take as much air out of the bag as possible and zip it. Refrigerate overnight. If you are in a hurry, you can serve the pickled cucumber after a minimum of 1 hour. However, leave it to marinate longer to allow the shio koji to soak deeper into the cucumber.

Serve without washing the shio koji off; just take it out of the bag and cut it into bite-size chunks or thick slices, then transfer it to an airtight jar. The pickled cucumbers should last a few days in the fridge.

fresh shio koji–marinated seafood poke bowl

Poke bowls are a really popular Hawaiian/Japanese dish. The shio koji makes the fish soft and tender, which makes it easier to eat raw.

yield: 2 servings

7 oz (200 g) sashimi-grade tuna or salmon

2 tbsp (30 g) Homemade Shio Koji (page 126)

3 cups (560 g) cooked short-grain Japanese koshihikari rice

1 avocado, sliced

Finely chopped scallions or shiso leaves, for garnish

Sesame seeds, for garnish

2 tsp (10 g) grated ginger root

1 tsp soy sauce, to serve, optional

1 tsp wasabi, to serve, optional

Cut the tuna into small cubed chunks and place it into a ziplock bag with the shio koji. Zip up the bag and massage the koji well into the fish. Unzip it to take as much air out as possible, then close the bag tightly and refrigerate the fish for 2 hours to let it marinate.

Divide the rice into two separate large rice bowls. Top them with the sliced avocado and divide the marinated tuna onto the rice. Scatter the scallions and sesame seeds over the tuna and top with the ginger. Mix soy sauce and wasabi for serving, if desired.

cozy vegetable soup with shio koji

This is a healthy and warming soup that's easy to make. I like to eat this for a light dinner and pack some for lunch the following day. The shio koji adds its own semi-salty flavor so you only need to season with a bit of pepper.

yield: 2 servings

1¼ cups (300 ml) Dashi with Bonito Flakes and Kelp (page 168)

1 tbsp (15 g) Homemade Shio Koji (page 126)

1 tbsp (15 ml) sake

½ cup (60 g) diced daikon radish

½ cup (60 g) diced carrot

1 cup (130 g) diced purple sweet potato

1 cup (160 g) diced onion

½ cup (50 g) parboiled broccoli, cut small

Pepper, to taste

Finely chopped scallions, for garnish

Bring the dashi to a boil in a pot over medium heat. Add the shio koji and sake and combine them. Add the daikon, carrot, sweet potato and onion and simmer for 20 minutes or until all vegetables are cooked and softened. Add the broccoli and cook for a further 3 minutes. Sprinkle it with pepper to taste and turn the heat off. Serve the soup in a soup bowl and garnish it with scallions.

multipurpose shio koji dressing with simple garden salad

This is an easy-to-make dressing that you can use to season salads and vegetables. I usually eat this with a very basic salad to give the vegetables more flavor.

yield: ⅓ cup (75 ml)

dressing

2 tbsp (30 g) Homemade Shio Koji (page 126)

1 tbsp (15 ml) olive oil

1 tbsp (15 ml) rice vinegar (komezu)

1 tbsp (15 ml) honey

Pinch of salt and pepper

salad

5 cherry tomatoes

¼ small English or Lebanese cucumber, sliced

1 cup (35 g) lettuce

1 tbsp (15 g) bean sprouts

To make the dressing, place the shio koji, olive oil, rice vinegar, honey, salt and pepper in a small mixing bowl and whisk to blend them well.

Place the salad ingredients in a bowl and drizzle the salad dressing over it. You can double or triple the dressing recipe to make a bulk amount. It will keep for 3 months in the fridge.

shio koji–marinated chicken

The shio koji makes this pan-fried chicken so soft and succulent. It does such a great job of tenderizing the meat and making it juicy that you could even use chicken breast (which usually goes dry) in place of the thighs. I like to make this chicken for dinner, then pack the leftovers in a salad for lunch the next day.

yield: 4 servings

2 chicken thighs, with skin on

3 tbsp (45 g) Homemade Shio Koji (page 126)

Green salad leaves, cucumber and cherry tomatoes, to serve

Score the chicken thighs and open it up to make the thickness of the meat even. Poke the skin with a fork, then place the chicken thighs and the shio koji in a ziplock bag. Zip the bag and massage the chicken thighs through the bag. Marinate the chicken in the fridge for 20 minutes.

Heat a frying pan over medium heat. Place the chicken on the pan with the skin side down. You do not need to remove the shio koji marinade, but it can be easily burnt so be careful if you include it. Brown the skin side for about 5 minutes, until crisp. Remove any excess oil produced. Flip the meat over and cook the other side for another 5 minutes. Turn the heat off. Remove the chicken to a chopping board and slice it about ½ inch (1 cm) thick. Serve with green salad leaves, cucumber and cherry tomatoes.

amazing *Natto* recipes

Natto is a traditional Japanese food made from fermented soybeans that dates back many years. It is still popular today and has gained fame worldwide due to its unique smell, taste and texture. It has a pungent aroma and a sticky, gooey texture that makes it an acquired taste for many—you either love it or you hate it, but you must try it at least once! I didn't eat natto that often when I was growing up, but when I went back to visit my parents in Japan a few years ago, we learned that natto had become super popular and everyone was eating it for breakfast because of how healthy it is. It was one of those classic diet trends that I always get convinced to try, so I did. I ate plain natto every day for about a week, but nowadays I like to incorporate it into my diet through a variety of delicious dishes. Some of my favorites are Japanese Curry with Summer Vegetables and Natto (page 166) and Classic Fried Rice with Natto (page 158).

You can add natto in so many ways to get all the health benefits while toning down the flavor. Natto is a very nutritious food containing vitamins, probiotics and essential minerals. One half-cup (100 g) serving of natto contains 75 percent of the recommended daily intake of manganese, 48 percent of the RDI of iron and high percentages of the RDI of copper,

magnesium, calcium, potassium, zinc and vitamins C and K. And like the other fermented foods in this book, it is packed with probiotics, which are good for the gut and aid in healthy digestion. So even if you have tried it and you weren't a fan, you might want to give it another go because there are many ways that you can eat and enjoy natto while reaping the healthy benefits it provides.

Natto can be prepared at home or you can use store-bought. Historically, natto was made by wrapping boiled soybeans in rice straw, which naturally contains *Bacillus subtillis*. Nowadays, it is mass-produced to be available in polystyrene containers or, alternatively, you can use one pack of natto to make your own batch that you can continue to eat and use as a starter for homemade natto. It takes time and effort, but in the end, you can have your own supply of natto to eat on its own or add to other dishes to pack your body with healthy fermented nutrients.

basic natto

This is a recipe for classic natto that you can use in a variety of dishes. You will need a premade pack of natto or natto starter spores as a starter culture, but once you have that, the process isn't difficult, and you will have your own supply of natto to continue using as starter culture and to enjoy in many dishes.

yield: 1½ cups (380 g)
fermentation time: 24 hours

¾ cup (150 g) soybeans

1½ tbsp (20 g) store-bought natto

using natto starter spores (starter culture) to make natto: Most of the process is the same except for the substitution of the natto starter spores instead of store-bought ready-made natto. Dissolve half a spoonful of natto spores (using the tiny spoon that comes with the spores) into 1 teaspoon of sterilized water. Place the drained, cooked and hot soybeans in a sterilized yogurt maker or container, then spread the natto spore solution over it and mix with a sterilized spoon. Use the same process as above for the rest of the fermentation.

Wash the soybeans and soak them in a large bowl with 3 parts water and 1 part soybeans for 8 to 12 hours. In hot weather, it requires only 8 hours, whereas in winter it will need 12 hours to completely soak.

Drain the water and place the soybeans in a large pot. Fill the pot with just enough water to cover the soy beans and bring it to a boil. Turn the heat down to low and simmer for 9 to 10 hours. If you want to use a pressure cooker, follow your pressure cooker directions and pressure-cook for 30 minutes.

While the soybeans are being cooked, sterilize the fermenting equipment. I used a yogurt maker to set and control the temperature easily. If you don't have a yogurt maker, you could use an oven to incubate the soybeans. Place a spoon in a yogurt maker tub and pour in boiling water to fill it. Leave it for 5 minutes, then discard the water and let the tub and spoon dry. Stir the store-bought natto and place it at the bottom of the yogurt maker tub using the sterilized spoon. Drain the cooked soybeans and place them over the starter natto in the tub while the cooked soybeans are very hot. *Bacillus subtilis natto* is resistant to heat, so it will not die when it touches the hot soybeans. The reason for mixing it with hot soybeans is to avoid contamination from other bacteria. Place a gauze or cheesecloth over the tub. *Bacillus subtilis natto* is an aerobic bacterium that requires oxygen, so use a lid that has holes or leave it loose to allow the natto to breathe. Set the temperature at 104°F (40°C) and allow the soybeans to ferment for 24 hours.

After fermenting for 24 hours, stir well and transfer it to an airtight container. Cover it with gauze or cheesecloth secured with a rubber band and refrigerate to rest and age it for another 24 hours. It will keep for up to a week in the fridge and 1 month in the freezer.

chickpea natto

Natto can be made with other beans too, like black beans and chickpeas. These beans are easier to find in supermarkets than soybeans, and they have a similar result with a different texture and taste.

yield: 2 cups (380 g)

¾ cup (150 g) chickpeas

1 package natto starter spores

Wash the chickpeas. Soak the chickpeas in a large bowl with 3 parts water and 1 part chickpeas for 12 hours. Drain the water. Massage the chickpeas to loosen the hulls and remove them by hand. Place the chickpeas in a large pot, then fill the pot with water and bring it to a boil. Turn the heat down to low and simmer for 1 hour. If you use a pressure cooker, follow your pressure cooker directions and cook for 20 minutes.

While the chickpeas are cooking, sterilize the fermenting equipment. Place a spoon in a yogurt maker tub and pour in boiling water to fill it. (If you don't have a yogurt maker, you could use an oven.) Leave it for 5 minutes, then discard the water (except for 1 teaspoon) and let the tub and spoon dry. Dissolve ½ of the special spoonful of natto spores into 1 teaspoon of sterilized water and set it aside. Discard the cooking water and place the drained chickpeas in the yogurt maker tub while the chickpeas are very hot. Spread the natto spore solution over the chickpeas and mix using the sterilized spoon. Place gauze or cheesecloth over the tub. Use a lid that has holes or leave it loose to allow them to breathe because the natto requires enzymes. Set the temperature at 105°F (40°C) and allow the chickpeas to ferment for 24 hours.

After they have fermented for 24 hours, stir them well and transfer them to an airtight container. Cover with gauze or cheesecloth and secure it with a rubber band, then refrigerate to rest and age them for 24 hours. It will keep for a week in the fridge and 1 month in the freezer.

easy natto on rice

(natto gohan)

This is a simple and traditional Japanese breakfast. Natto goes so well with plain steamed rice, and you can add a cooked or raw egg on top.

yield: 1 serving

¼ cup (50 g) Basic Natto (page 150)

½ tsp soy sauce

½ tsp mirin

½ tsp mustard

Bonito flakes

1 cup (200 g) cooked short-grain Japanese koshihikari rice

A quail egg yolk or regular egg yolk, optional

Scallions, finely chopped

Combine the natto, soy sauce, mirin, mustard and bonito flakes well in a small mixing bowl. Place the rice into a rice bowl and top it with the natto mixture. Make a small well in the natto and drop the egg yolk into the well, if using. Garnish with the scallions. Stir to combine everything in the rice bowl and serve.

note: This is how Japanese people eat this but there are variations. Other topping suggestions are shredded seaweed and sesame seeds. If you don't like raw egg, it can be omitted or you can cook the whole egg before mixing it into the rice bowl.

crunchy natto tempura kakiage

Kakiage is a type of tempura using vegetables. The natto adds some nutty flavor and crunchy texture to the kakiage.

yield: 2 servings

1 onion, thinly sliced

½ carrot, cut into sticks

¼ sweet potato, cut into sticks

1 scallion, finely chopped

½ cup (75 g) all-purpose flour, divided

½ tsp salt, plus more to serve

½ cup (120 ml) water

¼ cup (50 g) Basic Natto (page 150)

Sesame or vegetable oil, for deep-frying

Place the onion, carrot, sweet potato and scallion in a bowl and coat them with 2 tablespoons (30 g) of flour. Set them aside. Place the remaining flour and salt in a separate bowl and pour in the water; mix them together, but try not to overmix or the batter may become glutinous.

Add the vegetables and natto to the tempura batter and fold it all in. Heat the oil in a deep frying pan to 340°F (170°C). Scoop ¼ cup (60 g) of the mixture with a ladle, a pair of chopsticks or other utensil, then set the scoop into the oil gently so that it stays together in one clump. When the vegetables are cooked and golden brown, remove them from the oil and rest them on a wire rack. Serve with salt.

classic fried rice with natto

Cooking fried rice with natto is one of my favorites because it brings a flavorful nutty taste to plain rice and subdues the strong flavor of the natto. I always make more than enough sushi rice than I need for a meal and use the leftovers to cook fried rice. It's a great way to easily use leftovers to make a delicious dish.

yield: 2 servings

2 cups (400 g) cooked short-grain Japanese koshihikari rice

1 tbsp (15 g) Japanese mayonnaise

2 eggs

¼ cup (50 g) Basic Natto (page 150)

1 tsp soy sauce

½ tsp mirin

½ tbsp (7 ml) olive oil

1 tbsp (15 g) finely chopped scallions

Salt and pepper, to taste

In a small bowl, mix the cooked rice well with the mayonnaise. Place the eggs, natto, soy sauce and mirin in a mixing bowl. Mix them well and set it aside.

Heat the olive oil in a frying pan over high heat, then add the rice and fry it for a few minutes. Put the rice to one side of the pan, add the eggs and natto mixture to the empty space in the pan, then scramble the eggs. Once the eggs are half-cooked, stir them into the rice. When it is all mixed and fried well, add the scallions and stir. Salt and pepper to taste. Remove from the heat and serve.

natto warship roll sushi

(gunkan maki)

This type of sushi is called gunkan maki in Japanese because it is shaped like a warship. There are many different types of fillings for gunkan maki, and natto is a common one.

yield: 12 rolls

½ cup (100 g) Basic Natto (page 150)

1 tsp soy sauce

½ tsp mirin

¼ tsp mustard

2 cups (400 g) Sushi Rice (page 169)

2 sheets nori seaweed, cut into 12 strips

1½ tbsp (22 g) chopped scallions

Place the natto, soy sauce, mirin and mustard in a small mixing bowl and stir well. Set it aside.

Divide the sushi rice into 12 equal balls, about 3 tablespoons (40 g) each, and form each ball into an oval cylinder shape. Wrap the outside edge of each sushi with nori seaweed strips. The ends of the nori sheets will overlap, so glue them together with a grain of sushi rice. Fill the top gap of each sushi rice "warship" with 2 teaspoons (6 g) of the natto mixture. Top with chopped scallions.

refreshing natto and grated daikon soba noodle

This is so good to eat in the summer because the cold noodles cool you down and the grated daikon brings a nice, refreshing crunch to the dish. This dish can also be enjoyed warm in the colder months.

yield: 2 servings

²/₃ cup (80 g) Basic Natto (page 150)

2 tbsp plus ½ tsp (33 ml) soy sauce, divided

2 tbsp plus ½ tsp (33 ml) mirin, divided

½ tsp mustard

1 cup (250 ml) Dashi with Bonito Flakes and Kelp (page 168)

⅓ lb (150 g) soba noodles

½ cup (60 g) daikon, grated with the liquid squeezed out slightly

2 tbsp (30 g) finely chopped scallions

Shredded nori seaweed, for garnish

Combine the natto, ½ teaspoon soy sauce, ½ teaspoon mirin and mustard together in a small mixing bowl and set it aside.

To prepare the soup, place the dashi, 2 tablespoons (30 ml) soy sauce and 2 tablespoons (30 ml) mirin in a small saucepan and bring it to a boil over high heat. Once it has boiled, remove it from the heat. Put the soup in the refrigerator to cool until the noodles are ready.

Cook the noodles in a pot of boiling water until al dente, for about 3 minutes. Drain the cooking water. Rinse the noodles under cold running water, then drain them. Serve the noodles in a large bowl topped with grated daikon, natto and scallions. Then pour the cooled soup over the noodles and toppings. Sprinkle with the shredded nori seaweed.

natto avocado rice bowl

This rice bowl (donburi) is one of my favorite Japanese dishes because it's so easy to make and really filling. The nutty bean flavor of the natto and the creaminess of the avocado go so well together.

yield: 2 servings

¼ cup (50 g) Basic Natto (page 150)

½ avocado, diced

Shiso leaves, finely chopped

1½ tbsp (22 g) Japanese mayonnaise

3 cups (600 g) cooked short-grain Japanese koshihikari rice

Shredded nori seaweed, for garnish

Toss the natto, avocado, shiso leaves and mayonnaise all together in a mixing bowl and set it aside. Divide the rice into two large rice bowls. Divide the natto mixture evenly onto each rice bowl. Garnish with the shredded seaweed.

japanese curry with summer vegetables and natto

This dish combines the semisweet flavor of Japanese curry with the unique flavor of natto. My favorite topping for this curry is Worcestershire sauce, which is readily available and a popular curry topping in some regions of Japan—it's something that you have to try.

yield: 4 servings

1 tbsp (15 ml) olive oil

½ onion, finely chopped

2½ cups (600 ml) water

3½ oz (100 g) curry roux

Sesame or vegetable oil, for deep-frying

1 cup (120 g) frozen lotus root (renkon), or 4-inch (10-cm) fresh lotus roots, peeled and sliced to ¼ inch (5 mm) thick

1 red capsicum/red bell pepper, cut into bite-size pieces

1 eggplant, cut into ¼-inch (5-mm) slices

¼ cup (30 g) Kabocha squash, cut into ¼-inch (5-mm) slices

8 okra pods, trimmed and cut in half, optional

⅔ cup (80 g) Basic Natto (page 150)

2 tsp (10 ml) soy sauce

6 cups (1.2 kg) cooked short-grain Japanese koshihikari rice

Heat the olive oil in a pot and cook the onion until it becomes soft. Add the water to the pot and bring it to boil. Turn the heat off, add the curry roux and stir. Put the pot back on low heat and simmer to thicken the curry slightly. While the curry simmers, heat the sesame oil in a deep frying pan, then deep-fry the lotus root, pepper, eggplant, squash and okra, if using. When the color of the vegetables becomes brighter, remove them from the pan and set them to drain on a wire rack.

Place the natto and soy sauce in a small mixing bowl and stir. Serve the rice in a shallow bowl and pour the curry sauce on the side of the rice. Place the deep-fried summer vegetables in the bowl and top them with the natto and soy sauce mixture.

note: Japanese curry roux, or curry sauce mix, can be found online or in most supermarkets.

japanese cooking essentials

dashi with bonito flakes and kelp

Dashi is an essential in Japanese cooking—in fact, many Japanese dishes cannot be made without using it. This recipe will be needed as a base for Root Vegetable Miso Soup (page 13) and other dishes throughout the book.

yield: 4 cups (1 L)

1½ tbsp (8 g) kelp

4 cups (1 L) water

1½ tbsp (3 g) bonito flakes

Wash the kelp with a damp kitchen cloth to remove any dust that may be on it. Place the water in a large stock pot and bring it to a boil. Turn the heat down and add the kelp. Simmer for 20 minutes. Remove the kelp from the pot. Turn the heat up again and bring it to a boil. Add the bonito flakes all at once. When it boils again, turn the heat off and remove the pot from the heat. Leave it until all the bonito sinks to the bottom of the pot—be patient and don't stir it! Drain the dashi stock into another container with a sieve lined with gauze or cheesecloth. Do not squeeze the liquid out as it will leave an astringent bitter taste in the dashi. Store the dashi in a jar, and it will keep in the refrigerator for about 3 days or for 3 months in the freezer.

white sauce

This white sauce is necessary for several of the recipes in this book, like stews and Rice Gratin with White Miso Sauce (page 26). It's quick and easy to make and can be stored and used for different dishes.

yield: 1 serving

3½ tbsp (50 g) butter

½ cup (70 g) all-purpose flour

2 cups (500 ml) milk

Place the butter and flour in a mixing bowl and microwave it for 2½ minutes. Take the bowl out of the microwave and stir well. Gradually add the milk while constantly stirring. Once all the milk is added, loosely cover the bowl with cling wrap and microwave it for 3 minutes. Take the bowl out of the microwave and stir well. Put the cling wrap back on it loosely and microwave for another 2 minutes. Remove it from the microwave, stir it well again. It is ready to use for dishes or can be stocked in the fridge.

sushi rice

This is how I make sushi rice from scratch by making the sushi vinegar at home. You can use store-bought sushi vinegar instead, if you prefer. The best rice to use when making sushi is a short-grain Japanese koshihikari rice.

yield: 4½ cups (840 g) cooked rice

rice

1½ cups (300 g) uncooked short-grain Japanese koshihikari rice

1½ cups (360 ml) water

2-inch (5-cm) strip kombu kelp

sushi vinegar

½ cup (120 ml) rice vinegar (komezu)

1½ tbsp (22 g) granulated or caster sugar

½ tsp salt

Rinse the rice three times or more until the washing water becomes semi-clear. Place the rice into your rice cooker and set it per its instructions with the water. Add the kelp to the rice cooker and cook the rice.

While the rice is being cooked, make the sushi vinegar. Combine the rice vinegar, sugar and salt in a small saucepan. Heat the vinegar mixture over medium heat. Once it boils and the sugar has dissolved, turn the heat off and let it cool.

When the rice is cooked, transfer the rice into a wooden sushi tub or a large bowl. Pour all the sushi vinegar over the rice. Stir the rice with a wooden spatula with a scooping and cutting motion to mix the vinegar into the rice evenly. At the same time, use a hand fan to evaporate the excess moisture. This makes the sushi rice shine.

acknowledgments

Elizabeth and I would first like to thank each other for the work we both put into creating this book—and for getting through every argument to finish it! We would also like to thank our friends and family both in Japan and Australia for their continued support and love, and a special thanks to our Japanese grandmothers and aunties who passed down their recipes and knowledge of Japanese cooking and fermentation to us. A big thank you must be given to anyone who has ever read and loved our blog because this would not be possible without your support. And lastly, we would like to thank everyone at Page Street Publishing for giving us this opportunity and helping us with every step along the way to make this book a reality.

about the authors

shihoko ura was born and raised in a small town in Japan called Hikigawa. Like most children in Japan, she grew up eating fermented foods like miso as part of her meals every day. After having her daughter Elizabeth and her son James, she relocated to Australia where she found it much harder to find Japanese ingredients and fermented condiments to use in cooking. So she started to make her own. After discovering her passion for fermented foods, food photography and Japanese cooking, she and Elizabeth started the Japanese food blog, Chopstick Chronicles. The two collaborate on the blog with Shihoko doing the cooking and photos and Elizabeth doing the writing and editing.

elizabeth mcclelland loves to learn Japanese cooking from her mum, and they both enjoy using fermented ingredients in their cooking every day.

index